Stories of
GREAT PHYSICIANS

by
Raymond F. Jones

illustrated by
Shannon Stirnweis

WHITMAN PUBLISHING COMPANY, Racine, Wis.

Contents

1

Out of Darkness

The Greek isle of Cos is a warm, sunny spot of land, where the Mediterranean winds stir pleasantly in the branches of the great plane trees. On this island, modern medical science was born almost 2,500 years ago.

It was born in the person of a Greek physician named Hippocrates in 460 B.C. If you visit Cos today, the guides will show you an ancient plane tree, whose great, spreading branches are propped to keep them from breaking, and they will show you a marble tablet which says that under this very tree Hippocrates taught his students four centuries before Christ was born.

The guides are probably wrong. It is doubtful

that the tree is this old. And no one could know whether this is the exact spot where Hippocrates held his school.

But it was sunny and warm on Cos twenty-five centuries ago, just as it is today, and the open air was as good as any place to hold a school. Under some such tree as this, Hippocrates gathered his students.

They came from all over the world—Egypt, Persia, Sicily, Judea—and they paid a substantial tuition to learn from the master physician in person. They considered themselves most fortunate to sit at his feet and hear his voice.

To Hippocrates, however, it seemed that no one came but the most ignorant and superstitious of the would-be physicians. Or were there no other kinds?

Take the young Thessalonian, for example. He was going to speak now and inject his witless beliefs into the discussion. Hippocrates wondered if he ought to be more severe and forbid them to speak. But that was not the way to teach, either.

"You speak as if there were several diseases," the Thessalonian said, "but all symptoms are signs of the same great disease. A man sickens and dies. That is all there is to it. One death. One disease. There can't possibly be more than one."

"How many sick men have you examined?" Hippocrates demanded. "One? A hundred? Have you sat by the bedside of a thousand dying men as I have? Tell me!"

"Well, I have read— It is said that—"

"Read nothing! Listen to no one—not even to me!" exclaimed Hippocrates. "Go to sick men to find out about sick men. Go to dying men to find out what they die of. Then you will know. But not until then.

"However, I will tell you of the things I have seen, and when you make your own observations, you can determine whether I have told the truth or not.

"I have seen a young man who should have been strong and robust, but who was weak and pale. On his hollow cheeks there was a bright flush that was strange. He coughed almost constantly, until he was all but shaken apart. Such men, I have found, do not die immediately; they die slowly. And if they do as I prescribe, and go to the hills to rest in the sunshine, they often do not die of this disease at all.

"Others I have seen, with great fever, pains in the chest and delirium of the mind, who will either die very quickly or they will begin to get well. It would do no good to send these away to rest on a sunny hillside, but these I give cool and nourishing drinks and require that they have much fresh air and rest in bed.

"Now, will you tell me that these two conditions are one and the same disease? Of course they are not! And this you must learn if you are to be physicians: Observe your patient and treat him according to his illness."

The Egyptian student stirred and opened his mouth to speak. Hippocrates could almost guess what was coming.

"Did you not send an offering of food for the sacred serpents?" the Egyptian said. "I have heard that this—"

Hippocrates groaned to himself. "Can't you understand," he said, "that the sacred serpents, the gods of stone and brass, the invisible demons of the night air—none of these have anything to do with the illness of your patients? What good would it do to send food for the sacred serpents?"

"So you have told us, master," said the Egyptian. "But while we prescribe the proper food, the herbs, the air, or the sunshine it would not hurt to follow our ancient ritual. It would not hurt to have the sacred serpents on our side."

"Yes, it would," said Hippocrates, more slowly and thoughtfully now. "Every time you feed the sacred serpents, every time you bow to the gods of brass and stone, you lessen your own powers of healing. You say to yourself that it doesn't matter if you are uncertain of your observations, or wrong in your prescriptions. You say that the sacred serpents will appeal to Aesculapius and he will heal your patient in spite of your mistakes. No, you must learn that Aesculapius and all the stone gods are dead. Their priests are fools.

"You will learn that disease belongs to the order of nature. It is only by observing and obeying the laws of nature that you will find cures for your patients. And if nature resists, all measures are in vain."

So Hippocrates taught in an age when sick men still appealed to the sacred serpents of Aesculapius and prayed to stone gods for healing.

Hippocrates was the son of a doctor named Heracleides. He studied under his father and other instructors. He learned the philosophy and the arts of his time. But it was not long until those who knew him recognized something different in him.

Something new came into the world with Hippocrates. Other scientists, philosophers, artists, and political leaders shared it, too. Because of these men, the age in which they lived came to be known as the Golden Age of Greece. Hippocrates and his fellow Greeks brought into the world a new way of thinking, a kind of thinking that explained the world in terms of nature and made man responsible for his own welfare instead of assuming him to be the plaything of the gods of the sun and the wind and the forest.

Hippocrates surged forward on the first wave of this new experience of mankind. With it, he brought medicine out of the nightmare of superstition and fear in which it had lain since the dawn of human life.

But medical science was in its very infancy. Almost nothing was known of the anatomy of human organs, although the skeleton was fairly well understood. It was forbidden to dissect the human body. Medicines were developed after long trial and error. Some of them relieved illness and injury. Some of them did more harm than good. Some surgical operations were performed, but anesthetics were not to be discovered until almost our own time.

Hippocrates is the first physician of whom we have any knowledge who observed his patients carefully and made an accurate record of their symptoms and conditions, and treated them accordingly. If this seems like a small accomplishment, remember that it was the custom to regard all diseases as one and to feed the sacred serpents to obtain a cure.

On the basis of his case histories, Hippocrates predicted the course of many diseases for the first time, and prescribed useful treatment. After the

Golden Age, no physician again made such accurate observations for eighteen hundred years.

Hippocrates was the first to discover and teach the great need to work with natural processes of the body in healing, and for this his name has come to represent all that is great and enlightened in the science of medicine.

After completing his studies on Cos, Hippocrates journeyed to many distant places. It was the custom for doctors to travel from city to city and to offer their services as they went. The reputation of Hippocrates went before him. His methods showed results beyond anything the magicians and the priests could produce. In a new city he would be received with great welcome. The sick would gather and plead for his assistance.

Many stories are told of his travels. Some of them are legends that grew up long after he was dead. Others are based on fact. We have little means of knowing which is which.

According to these stories he traveled to Macedonia and was called to the bedside of the sick king. The court physicians had diagnosed the illness

as consumption, and for this Hippocrates would
have prescribed long rest in a sunny location. But
he shook his head after examining the king.

"The illness of your king is not consumption,"
he told the members of the court. "The illness he
suffers is an illness which the mind brings upon the
body. He is disturbed in his thoughts, and he broods
upon things that are long past. From this has his
sickness come."

So Hippocrates may be credited with recognizing
what we today call psychosomatic illness, the illness
of the body which is caused by mental disturbances.

A former teacher of Hippocrates, the philosopher
Democritus, became insane and Hippocrates was
sent for by the people of the city of Abdera, where he
lived. They also asked Hippocrates to free their city
of a great plague. The stories do not tell us the outcome of these requests.

In the city of Athens at another time a plague
also raged. Hippocrates observed that blacksmiths
were immune to the plague and concluded that the
nearness of their hot fires kept the plague away—
he knew absolutely nothing, of course, of germs or

sterilization. When the epidemic was reduced, the Athenians erected a statue with a plaque that said, "To our rescuer and benefactor Hippocrates." He was made a citizen of Athens, the city's highest honor.

As his fame grew, the King of Persia, Artaxerxes, offered him great sums of money to come to Persia as court physician. Hippocrates wrote back to the king, "Your offer does a humble physician of Greece a great honor, but the needs of my own people make it impossible for me to commit my life and services elsewhere."

Besides, the Persians were the traditional enemies of Greece.

Hippocrates died in Thessaly at a very advanced age. Some records give his age as ninety-four; some give it as high as one hundred and ten. At least, he was very old when he died.

A final legend is attached even to his tombstone. It was said that a swarm of bees built their hive over his grave and that the honey from this hive would cure children of an illness called thrush.

During his lifetime, Hippocrates wrote con-

stantly—medical texts, letters, articles, case histories and philosophical essays. These writings were
scattered all over Greece at the time of his death.
In the third century B.C. they were collected.

Then it was found that others writings were mixed
with his. His fame became so great after his death
that every good medical writing—and many poor
ones—came to be attributed to him. Some made
exactly opposite statements. Scholars are uncertain,
even today, as to whether some of these manuscripts
were or were not written by Hippocrates.

The most famous of the Hippocratic writings is,
of course, the Hippocratic Oath. Generations of
medical students, at the completion of their studies,
have stood in their graduating halls and recited this
Oath. Unfortunately, it was not written by Hippocrates. It originated before his time, but because
of his fame, and because it expressed so well the
things for which he stood, the name of Hippocrates
became connected with it. And it may well be taken
to represent his thoughts and his life.

This Oath says in part: "I swear . . . to reckon
him who taught me this art equally dear to me as

my parents, to share my substance with him, and relieve his necessities if required. . . . I will follow that . . . which . . . I consider for the benefit of my patients, and abstain from whatever is deleterious and mischievous. I will give no deadly medicine to anyone if asked. . . . With purity and holiness I will pass my life and practice my art. Whatever . . . I see or hear . . . which ought not to be spoken of abroad, I will not divulge. While I continue to keep this Oath unviolated, may it be granted to me to enjoy life and the practice of the art, respected by all men, in all times. But should I trespass and violate this Oath, may the reverse be my lot."

In his own writings, Hippocrates spoke of the importance of the dress and behavior of the physician. He wrote, "When the physician enters the room of the patient he should be attentive to the manner in which he sits down and the manner in which he comports himself; he should be well dressed, have a calm face, give the patient his entire attention, answer objections calmly and not lose patience, and be calm in the presence of difficulties that arise. The most important rule is to repeat his examinations frequently to avoid mistakes; he should keep aware of the fact that patients often lie when they state that they have taken certain medicines. All the directions of the physician should be made in a friendly, quiet manner. Naught should be betrayed to the patient of what may happen . . . because many patients have been driven in this way to extreme measures. Where there is love of man, there is also love for the art."

This shows a kindly man, whom we would greatly welcome at our own bedside in time of illness. It is no wonder that his own generation and those that

followed loved him and revered him.

In his writings are found many philosophical and medical sayings which have become famous in all lands:

"Life is short and art is long, the occasion fleeting, experience fallacious, and judgment difficult."

"To know is science, but merely to believe one knows is ignorance."

"The forces of nature are the physicians of disease."

The principles that Hippocrates taught are so common today that it is sometimes difficult to recognize what a tremendous change he brought about in men's thinking concerning medicine and healing. He was the first to sit patiently at the bedside of sick men and women and learn the symptoms of illness, the first to describe accurately diseases of the body and mind. With the limited medical knowledge of his day he devised treatments that were in harmony with nature. He loved the art of healing, and he loved mankind.

Behind Hippocrates we see the ghostly shadows

of witch doctors sitting in smoky caves with bear skins over their shoulders, claws on their hands, and animal horns on their heads. Before them is a sick child from whom they try to drive out a devil so the child may be well.

We see people so terrified by illness that they drag their sick into the open fields to die rather than contaminate the village by their deaths. We see the temples of Aesculapius and the sacred serpents that must be fed so the sick will be healed. We see the priests of ancient Egypt with their incense and their sacrifices.

Before them all stands Hippocrates, who told them their day was over, that from his time forward sick men would be treated with logic and reason and the powers of nature, that no more would they be tormented with superstition and useless magic.

Hippocrates, the Father of Medicine, brought the medical world out of darkness into light.

2

A Dream Comes True

Galen, the son of Nicon, was home again. It had been a long nine years since he had last set eyes on Pergamum, the place of his birth, and it was good to be back. Good, too, to know the respect and admiration of the people who had doubted him as a youth. He had shown them his father had not dreamed in vain.

He sat in the otherwise empty spectators' balcony overlooking the arena of the gladitorial school of Pergamum and watched the dozen pairs of battling gladiators below. The sun beat down in hot fury in the summer afternoon. Sweat stood out in glistening film on the bodies of the fighters. On more than half of them the sweat was mixed with the bright redness of their own blood, although the battles in the training school were not to the death.

Galen's eyes were drawn to a single pair in the center of the arena. Demos, the Thracian, was battling desperately with Ngath, the giant Nubian. These two had never been paired in the arena before, and the fierce enmity that had brewed between them the past months was spilling over now. Theirs was no game. Each was fighting for his life.

Galen knew the folly of permitting himself friendship with the gladiators, but he had come to know Demos well. He didn't want him to die at the hands of the Nubian.

But Demos was weakening. Blood covered his right leg from a great wound in his side. He stumbled and almost fell, avoiding the Nubian's onslaught only by taking a mighty blow on his shield. Galen looked around desperately. Where was that idiot, Martinus, the arena master? He was supposed to stop such battles as these.

The arena master was suddenly there, shouting and screaming at the top of his lungs. All the other combatants ceased their struggles and stood apart.

But Ngath and Demos seemed not to have heard.

Martinus slammed the flat of his sword against the huge back of the Nubian. Ngath continued his slashing attack on Demos.

"Separate them!" Martinus commanded the other gladiators.

A dozen swords were thrust between the battling pair. Demos and Ngath slashed at them, trying to turn them aside to continue their struggle against each other.

Slowly, the pair was separated and disarmed. In frenzied rage, Martinus ordered the gladiators back to their quarters. Demos had to be carried. He had fainted from the loss of blood.

Then Martinus shouted hoarsely, "Galen! Dr. Galen, where are you?" He spat dust and blood and took up the cry again. "Galen! Dr. Galen—!"

Galen made no reply. He got up slowly and moved down to the cool, stone corridors of the gladiators' quarters.

Demos was scarcely conscious. "It's too late," he said. "The Nubian has finished me. I let him trick me into getting too angry. Did you see him? He

fights like a throwing engine. He was born only to kill. He could never love or laugh or see beauty —just kill. That's why I have to kill him. Now, it's too late—"

"Shut up," Galen said. "You're as big a fool as Martinus, letting Ngath draw you on that way. But you're far from dead. I've never lost a gladiator yet."

The wounds were great, but Galen thought no vital organs had been pierced, or major blood vessels cut. If only it were possible to know for sure where the vital organs and blood vessels were!

He cursed the lack of knowledge and the ignorance that prevented doctors from finding out what was in the human body. A doctor had to do the best he could with the knowledge he had. Galen dressed the wound of Demos with all the skill he had learned in his long years of study and his travels to the medical centers of the world. He meant to keep clear his record that no wounded gladiator should ever die under his care. It was a tough record to keep, with fighters like Ngath and Demos!

Besides, he liked Demos.

But he'd better take a look at Ngath, too. The

Nubian hadn't escaped without his share of wounds.

The post of physician to the gladiators was one eagerly sought by all doctors, and Galen was envied by his fellow physicians. The job paid well, and it offered great opportunity for practical experience! Besides caring for injuries, the physician controlled the physical exercise and diet of the gladiators.

But Galen was restless, as always. He wanted to stay and he wanted to go. He loved Pergamum, where he had spent his youth. It brought back memories of his father, Nicon, the architect and engineer, to whom he had been so close. Nicon had been a quiet, gentle man, in contrast to Galen's bitter, shrewish mother. Nicon had named his son in apparent longing for the quiet and peace that was denied him in his home. The Greek word *galenos* means calm and describes the smoothness of a sea undisturbed by wind or waves. Nicon educated his son carefully, and when Galen was eighteen, Nicon had a dream which led him to educate Galen as a physician. Then, when Galen was twenty, his beloved father died.

With two years of medical study behind him, and

nothing more to hold him at Pergamum, Galen began his tour of the world. He studied in Smyrna under leading physicians. He went to Greece. Finally, he reached Alexandria, Egypt, the leading center of knowledge of anatomy, which was Galen's special interest. At one time it had been possible to obtain human organs extracted from bodies prepared for embalming in Egypt. But that was long ago. Physicians now had to be content with dissection of animals, and in this, Galen excelled.

After returning to Pergamum at the age of twenty-eight, Galen resisted his wanderlust for three years. During this time he held the position of physician to the gladiators and maintained an extensive practice among the city's most notable people. He wrote much and continued his studies of anatomy.

Then he decided to take the big step: He would go to Rome, the capital of the world!

For an immigrant physician, life in Rome was not unlike life in a jungle. Doctors from all over the civilized world came to Rome to seek their fortunes among the great and the rich. Many were quacks and mere butchers, and the competition was deadly.

Galen was not especially dismayed by these conditions. He had inherited enough of his mother's competitive, quarrelsome character to make him quite willing to take on the physicians of Rome under their own terms.

One of his first moves was to call on his countrymen from Pergamum and make their acquaintance. Among these was an elderly philosopher of considerable reputation. His name was Eudemus.

Shortly after meeting Galen, Eudemus was taken ill with a severe fever. He did not call his new friend, Galen, but, rather, the most noted physician in Rome. Under this doctor's care, Eudemus grew rapidly worse until he was not expected to live. Only then did he think of young Galen, with whom he had had some pleasant talks on philosophy.

Galen came and made his examination. He diagnosed the illness and predicted its course. He prescribed treatment. Eudemus recovered.

At a single stroke, Galen's reputation was established. Eudemus carried his name into the most fashionable and richest households of Rome. The rich and the learned sought Galen's services, and it became fashionable to be treated by him. But this success aroused the bitter enmity of the physicians who lost well-paying patients to him. They challenged him openly. Who was he, anyway? Who had ever heard of Dr. Galen before? To what school of medical thought did he belong?

Galen didn't mind the battle. He answered his critics readily. He belonged to no special school of medical thought. He was himself, Galen replied. He practiced according to the best knowledge of the time, wherever it could be found. He admitted to only one master, Hippocrates.

Within a miraculously short time Galen had almost reached the pinnacle of success in Rome. Several of his aristocratic friends wanted to recommend him to the Emperor Marcus Aurelius. Then a mysterious thing happened, which has never been explained by historians or by any of Galen's own writings.

Galen suddenly asked his friends not to mention his name to the emperor. He quietly sold all his goods and left Rome, almost secretly. He traveled on foot to a seaport on the eastern shore of Italy and took ship for Greece. From there he traveled on to Pergamum. He had been gone four years.

Galen may have fled Rome because of a great plague, which he saw was coming, and which was beyond the power of all the physicians to stop. If so, his flight was in vain, for the plague struck Pergamum, too. It is also possible that his enemies had threatened his life. The exact truth will probably never be known.

In Pergamum, Galen quietly resumed his work and his studies. He dissected and wrote his observations in every spare moment. But his fame in Rome was not forgotten by one very important person. Within a short time, Galen received a message from the emperor himself, commanding him to return. Galen responded, but not in any great hurry. He joined the emperor's court almost two years after he had fled Rome.

Galen became the personal physician and close friend of Marcus Aurelius. The emperor is almost better known as a great philosopher and scholar than as the ruler of the Roman Empire. He and Galen had many long and pleasant discussions about philosophy and other scholarly subjects.

Galen was not a humble man by any means. He was proud of his superior knowledge and medical skill and of his position at the Roman court. He saw no reason why he should not be proud. His attitude is shown by his reaction on one occasion when he was called to the emperor's bedside after Marcus Aurelius had done too much celebrating following a Roman military victory.

"Galen!" The emperor welcomed him to his chamber in an exhausted voice. "I am glad you have come. I am very ill, Claudius Galen. Feel my pulse and tell me what is wrong and what must be done."

It was scarcely necessary for Galen to feel the pulse, but he did as commanded. Then he shook his head. "Considering your age and normal state of health, Your Majesty, I find nothing wrong in your pulse. It seems to be quite normal."

"But I am ill! I cannot stand. I get dizzy and sick at my stomach even when I try to sit up."

"The difficulty lies in your stomach," said Galen. "I would say you have consumed far more food than your stomach required in the past day or two.

The food lies heavy and resists digestion."

"That's it!" The emperor cried. "That's it! That's the very thing that has happened. I did eat far too much night before last, and drank much beyond the point of wisdom. What is to be done? I have business of the State that cannot wait. Yet here I lie like an aging dog. You must give me a remedy, Galen."

"For ordinary patients," said Galen, "I always prescribe a glass of wine sprinkled with pepper. But to be cautious and safe for a king, I prescribe some wool to be soaked in warm spikenard and laid over your stomach as a soothing bandage. This will quiet the disturbance and cause the food to be digested and pass on."

"Excellent! I shall have the wool and warm spikenard brought at once." The emperor turned to his aide. "Pitholaus, you have heard the prescription of Dr. Galen. Bring the materials and apply them at once!"

The following day, Galen called again at the palace and inquired of Pitholaus how the emperor was feeling.

"Wonderful!" exclaimed Pitholaus. "He applied

the wool and spikenard as you prescribed, and he also drank a glass of wine sprinkled with pepper for good measure. His health is much improved, and he is full of warm praise for you."

"He is? What does he say of me?" Galen asked eagerly.

"He says he has only one physician and, at last, an honest one."

Galen was very careful in his writings to record the high opinion of the emperor and others whom he treated, opinions which were quite in accord with Galen's own. Hippocrates would not have bothered with such trifling information.

Galen has been criticized by later generations for his proud and haughty attitude, for his quarrelsome independence and unceasing attacks on his fellow physicians. He has been criticized for jumping to conclusions that were not supported by facts and for his lack of careful bedside observations.

Some of this may be excused as the jungle-like attacks by lesser physicians of Rome. Some may be excused as the impatience of a man of genius with ordinary men and ordinary things. However, some may not be excused at all.

But Galen was a superior physician, standing head and shoulders above others of his time. Much of his superiority was the result of his intense, life-long interest in anatomy. One of his foremost cases, which stirred all Rome, is the direct result of this.

A noted Persian philosopher, visiting in Rome, lost the sense of feeling in the fourth and fifth fingers and half of the middle finger of one hand. The Persian called some of the most noted physicians of Rome, who applied ointments and other treatments to the affected fingers. These treatments produced no results. Galen was called.

He listened to the story of the Persian's condition and scarcely looked at the man's fingers. "Have you recently suffered any injuries of the arm?" he asked.

"Not of the arm," said the Persian, thinking back over recent days, "but I did fall and strike my back, between the shoulders, on a sharp stone."

"Ah, that is it," said Galen. "We will cure the injury to your back, and then your fingers will be well."

The Persian was astonished at this prediction,

and his other physicians were angered by what they considered Galen's ignorance.

Galen answered their objections very patiently —for him. He said, "The nerve which goes to the last two fingers and half of the middle finger branches out in the seventh cervical vertebra. Therefore, I look for an injury to this nerve when these fingers cannot feel. The patient says he has hurt his back. I find an injury which has caused inflammation of the spinal cord and damage to the nerve leading to these fingers. I will apply remedies to the patient's back and make his fingers well."

"If what you say is true," his opponents exploded, "this man could not move his fingers. Yet he moves them very well. How little you know of medicine!"

"It is you who know little," said Galen. "Otherwise, you would understand that there are separate nerves for the muscles and the skin. If only the former are injured, there is loss of movement, but not of feeling. If the latter, there is loss of feeling, but not of movement. You can learn of this in my books on anatomy, if you care to."

Anatomy had come a long way since the time of

Hippocrates, when little or no distinction was made between nerves, blood vessels, and certain muscle tissue. Yet in neither Greece nor Rome was the dissection of human bodies permitted. Galen felt this was no great obstacle, however. He considered the bodily structures of human beings and of animals to be very much alike.

Galen was not a patient bedside observer like Hippocrates, but he acknowledged his debt to the Father of Medicine. He was the first systematic experimental researcher in medicine. He was sometimes hasty, sometimes drawing unjustified conclusions that led to error. But he was the first to point medicine in the direction of new experimental work.

Galen lived out the remainder of his life in Rome and died at about the age of seventy.

He is thought to have produced over five hundred books, but many were lost in a disastrous fire at his home in Rome. We know today of approximately eighty.

All his life, Galen took deep pride in his superiority as a physician and experimenter. In later years he wrote, "I have continued my practice on until old age, and never as yet have I gone far astray whether in treatment or in prognosis, as have so many other doctors of great reputation. If anyone wishes to gain fame through these, and not through clever talk, all that he needs is, without more ado, to accept what I have been able to establish by zealous research."

Unfortunately for science, the physicians of later generations took these last words of Galen all too seriously. They were quite content to take his word as final for everything pertaining to anatomy. For centuries afterward, no one spent long hours over the dissecting table as he had done.

Yet Galen did not teach that men should cease to investigate and experiment. He did not claim there was no more to be known. He cannot be blamed that others set up his work as the standard for centuries to come and ceased to think at all for themselves.

Galen lived at the end of a dying era, and after his time a night of intellectual darkness settled over all the world. No more discoveries in medicine or any other field of science were made for hundreds of years. But the darkness was not quite as great as it was before Hippocrates, for the simple reason that men like Hippocrates and Galen had lived in the world, and no amount of darkness could change that fact.

3

The Anatomist

The town gates were locked behind him. Formless night shadows mingled under the moonless sky. Although the night breeze was not cold, Andreas Vesalius drew his collar a bit closer about his throat. He shivered a little as he waited under the dark limbs of an ancient tree and wondered if a thing like this was worth the risk of his neck.

Midnight.

At last he moved slowly away from the town, clinging to the darkest shadows beside the road. There had been no sign of any other person during the past two hours, but he glanced warily from side to side.

Ahead of him lay the bleak outline of gallows

hill. A corpse or two could be seen swinging faintly from the gibbets in the night wind. Vesalius glanced over his shoulder again and fingered his collar nervously. If he should be caught in this night's venture, his own corpse would soon swing there, also.

Alert for anyone else who might be fool enough to be abroad in such a place at such a time, he climbed the slope of the hill. It was only a short distance and soon he stood at the crest, beside the prize he sought.

White, even in the darkness of the night, a perfect skeleton hung in chains against a high post. Through recent days, the birds had picked the skeleton clean, and now it hung in almost perfect condition for transfer to the anatomist's study.

Taking a deep breath, Vesalius laid his hands upon the bones and began pulling them apart. He laid them carefully on the ground in a neat pile. To get at the upper ones he had to build a support of logs piled nearby for construction of the next gibbet. The chains held some of the bones tightly and Vesalius broke out in sweat as he twisted them from side to side, to free them from the fetters.

In spite of all his precautions, the metallic clank of the chains rang out in the stillness of the night. He imagined they must sound as loud as the church bell in the town. He clung to them to still their sound. His heart pounded furiously.

But at last he stepped to the ground with the final bit of the prize in his hand. He scooped the bones carefully into a sack he had brought with him and moved as fast as he dared down the slope of the hill. Behind him, the empty chains gave a faint rattle as the wind nudged them.

Vesalius moved back along the road toward the town. A few hundred yards from the town wall he turned and made his way through thick brush. The sack of bones was far too large to attempt to smuggle through the gates at one time. At the base of a tree in a tiny clearing he dug a shallow hole and covered the bones with earth. Only a handful of small ones he concealed in his pockets. Then he sat down beside the trunk of the tree to await daylight. He began to breathe easier. He had made it, he thought. He had really made it!

Anatomical specimens were hard to obtain, even in the sixteenth century. In Paris, a dissection was held occasionally, but it was a poor performance. Sitting at the base of the tree in the morning twilight, Andreas Vesalius thought of his classes back in Paris. Old Professor Sylvius had taught one of them. With a book of Galen in one hand and a scalpel in the other, he performed dissections on the bodies of dogs. When the dog's anatomy didn't agree with Galen it was too bad for the dog. The dog was obviously wrong.

"You can plainly see," Professor Sylvius said, "how the dog has changed since the days of Galen. However, you will understand that the way Galen describes it is the way the dog *should* be."

Again, when one of the rare dissections on a human body had shown that the hip bones of a man did not flare widely as Galen described them, it was said, "The change in the shape of a man's hip bones since the time of Galen is obvious. This may be attributed to the custom of wearing tight trousers instead of the loose togas, which was the custom in ancient times. You will observe how correct

Galen is in every detail and how man has brought upon himself these distortions." It was more than a man could stomach, Vesalius thought.

He let his thoughts drift to his boyhood. He could not remember a time when he had not had a craving within him to understand the structure of living things. He remembered how he had built clever traps to catch mice and rats and moles for dissection. He had been twelve years old then.

His mother had held her nose when near his quarters, but his father had smiled fondly and encouraged his young son's explorations into the world of nature. He had helped young Andreas construct the water wings of pigs' bladders with which Andreas learned to swim. Vesalius remembered how he had wondered about the texture and elasticity of those organs.

Andreas Vesalius was born in Brussels in 1514, on the last day of the year. His place of birth was quite accidental. The family was of the town of Wesel on the Rhine, but his father was the apothecary of the imperial court of Margaret of Braband, and court was established in Brussels that winter.

The Vesalius family was a family of physicians.

Andreas had gone to school first at Louvain, outside whose walls he now waited for the dawn. But his father had wanted him to have the best of medical education. That meant Paris.

Paris had been a great disappointment. There had been old Professor Sylvius, and there had been Professor von Andernach. As a dissector, von Andernach was a great translator. He had translated Galen's work from Greek into Latin, but the only time he seemed to use a knife was at mealtimes.

There had been an occasional rare dissection of a human body. Because of his intense interest, Vesalius had attracted attention early in his classes. At the third human dissection he was asked to take part. He did very well and was asked to perform another dissection alone.

When war broke out, Vesalius left Paris to return to Louvain. Here, he determined to acquire for himself a complete human skeleton—regardless of the risk and cost to himself.

Well, he had his prize now, he thought. All that remained was to get it inside the walls of the town, to his own quarters. But that would be relatively simple. He would remove a bone or two at a time from the shallow grave. When it was all assembled in his rooms what envy he would arouse among his fellow medical students!

He waited until long after sunrise and people were moving freely in and out of the town gate, going to the fields outside or traveling to and from the nearby village. Cautiously, he stepped from hiding and strode along the road toward the gates. He nodded to the old woman selling flowers and moved on into the town, a whistle on his lips.

After many days the entire skeleton was recovered, the bones cleaned and assembled. Now, Vesalius displayed it proudly and openly to his admiring friends. He had brought it with him from Paris, he said. Who could say he had not? Certainly no one could offer the slightest shred of proof— even if he had some suspicions—that the skeleton had once been chained to a post on gallows hill outside Louvain!

The enthusiasm of Vesalius inspired, at times, both his professors and his fellow students. With other students, he played a game of his own invention. They would take turns being blindfolded, and the others would hand the blindfolded student a human bone. He would attempt to identify it by feeling alone.

Vesalius was always the champion. They handed him the most difficult bones.

"This one, Andreas?" said his friend, Regnier Gemma.

Vesalius laughed beneath his blindfold. "That is far too easy. There is no other bone like the femur in the whole body. Why don't you give me a skull and ask me what it is?"

"All right, this one," said another student.

"The ulna," said Vesalius. "Give me some difficult ones. Let me feel the little bones of the fingers and the toes, the parts of the spine. Then I will show you how a blind man can be a doctor of anatomy!"

The medical school at Louvain was becoming more progressive in Vesalius' time. The last public dissection of a human body had taken place eighteen years before, but now the energetic Andreas Vesalius was invited to perform some. He dissected with great precision. He wrote abundant descriptions and drew sketches of the organs and structures he found.

What errors there were in the old books!

The human womb has two chambers, like horns, Galen had said. It simply wasn't so, Vesalius found. The human womb was a smooth, single chamber.

The breastbone. Galen said it had seven parts. There were only three.

The liver. Several lobes, Galen said. Vesalius could not find them. And he did not believe—as Professor Sylvius did—that man had changed that much since the time of Galen.

The lower jaw was supposed to have two parts.

Then Vesalius knew the truth. Galen had never dissected a single human body in his whole life! He described the anatomy of pigs, sheep, and monkeys. He had assumed no difference in the anatomy of men. How wrong he had been!

Vesalius felt sorry for Galen. The great man had pointed the way to experimental medicine, but he had been so handicapped by the times in which he lived that he could no more than glimpse the true direction of the path that lay ahead. He could not be blamed for the errors men made in his name. He would have been the first to welcome a chance to correct his observations by human dissection. He would have been the first to laugh at old Sylvius and the theory of tight pants causing narrow hips.

But this error had to be corrected now, before any more wasted years elapsed, Vesalius thought furiously. And he was going to be the one to do it!

Although Vesalius enjoyed more freedom in Louvain than Galen had ever known in Greece and Rome, there was still considerable opposition to dissection of human bodies. The priests didn't like it, although they could no longer stop it. Dissection was no longer a heresy that could bring burning at the stake. But the priests were alert for the slightest slip on the part of medical students which could bring such a charge. Vesalius sensed they had set their traps for him. Their fingers itched to light a pile of faggots around him, as they had done to many other medical men who had not been too careful in their public statements.

Vesalius knew he had to find another place of

study and he had to find it quickly.

To the southeast, in Italy, the great medical center of Padua seemed the most logical place. He abandoned Louvain and set out for Padua.

On his way, he visited a friend in Basel, Switzerland, John Oporinus, who was a professor of Greek and also the owner of a fine printing press. Vesalius showed him the drawings and notes of his dissections, and John Oporinus agreed to publish a book for him. He gave Vesalius a letter of introduction to the University of Padua, and one to a fellow countryman, an artist pupil of Titian, Stephan Kalkar, who might be persuaded to make the final drawings from Vesalius' sketches.

Stephan Kalkar was found in Venice, and he, too, was won over by the enthusiasm of Andreas Vesalius for a great project which would give a correct description and illustration of human anatomy for the first time in history. Kalkar went on to Padua with Vesalius.

Vesalius continued his studies and received his doctor's degree at Padua in December of 1537. On completion of his examinations Vesalius offered

to demonstrate for the professors the game he had invented in Louvain. They agreed to watch his demonstration.

Blindfolded, he sat before them. With some doubt and hesitation they handed him a bone from the pile on a nearby table. Vesalius ran his sensitive fingertips over its surface.

"Shoulder blade," he said. That one was too easy, but the professors grunted in pleased admiration. They handed him another.

Vesalius examined it carefully on all sides with his fingertips. "A scaphoid bone of the ankle," he responded without any hesitation.

They gave him a third bone. He had played this game too often to be very worried about anything on which they could test him.

"Radius, from the forearm," he said confidently.

The professors exclaimed in pleased satisfaction and amazement.

The test continued through the long afternoon. When it was over, the professors conferred with each other for a long time. Then they announced a most important decision. The University of Padua had never had a professorship of anatomy, but they were willing to create one and give it to young Andreas Vesalius. He accepted without hesitation.

He was just twenty-three years old.

He now began a period of furious activity that few men have ever equaled. With Stephan Kalkar at his side, Vesalius spent the next four and a half years dissecting, analyzing, and studying the structure of the human body—in addition to his teaching duties, of course. Kalkar drew as Vesalius dissected. By August, 1542, they had their great project completed.

Vesalius had not forgotten the excellent printing and the promise of his friend John Oporinus. He wanted his great book to be a work of art in the printing. He loaded the precious blocks for the illustrations on pack mules and traveled with them to Switzerland.

The faculty of the University in Basel welcomed him, for his reputation had preceded him as a result of the small atlas and other writings which he had done. While overseeing the printing work, Vesalius delivered some lectures and dissected a body whose skeleton is still to be seen in the Anatomical Institute at Basel.

In June of 1543, the great anatomy book was printed and ready for distribution. It contained 663 pages of text and over three hundred of Stephan Kalkar's magnificent drawings.

Vesalius breathed a sigh of relief. The work was finished. Now he could return to Padua and resume his teaching and enjoy a far more leisurely life than he had known for a long time. He was twenty-eight, and he had accomplished far more than most men do in an entire lifetime.

But the expected peace did not come. Instead, a storm of incredible violence poured down upon the head of Vesalius.

"This is sacrilege!" the universities cried. "Vesalius has denied Galen. How can a man be allowed to teach physicians when he claims human anatomy is different from Galen's descriptions?"

True, many accepted his book with enthusiasm and gratitude that corrected information was now available. But in the universities the older professors were staunch followers of Galen, and Vesalius had committed a great crime in their sight.

Professor Sylvius would have none of it. He declared, "Man has changed since Galen's time, and not for the better."

Realdo Colombo, one of Vesalius' most brilliant and loyal students, turned against him when he saw how strong the tide of professional opinion moved against his master. He publicly denounced Vesalius.

Wearied and exhausted by his long years of intense labor, Vesalius could not endure the attacks for long. In a state of depression he burned many unpublished manuscripts, left Padua and Italy behind him, and looked for work elsewhere.

He turned to Spain, where he was offered an appointment as court physician to Charles V, emperor of most of the known world at that time. It was a place of high honor and of safety from the attacks of the swarm of little men with little minds.

Vesalius' great contribution had been made. He did no more scientific work. For twenty years he was court physician in Spain. Then a series of mysterious circumstances shrouded the last months of his life.

He suddenly left Madrid in 1564. No one knows just why. There is one story that he had attended the final illness of a young Spanish nobleman. When the young man died, Vesalius asked the parents' consent to perform an autopsy to discover the exact cause of death. On opening the body, Vesalius found the heart still beating faintly. When this was reported to the Inquisition, only the emperor could save Vesalius from burning at the stake, and this was done on the condition that he take a journey of penance to the Holy Land.

Some say there is no truth to this story, that he

was merely tired of court life, that he was homesick for Italy, that he decided to visit Jerusalem for his health.

At any rate, Vesalius crossed the Alps and was in Italy once more. The chair of anatomy at Padua was vacant because of the death of Fallopius, who had taken it when Vesalius left twenty years before. The position may have been offered to Vesalius again. He may have intended to return and accept it.

But he continued his journey and visited Jerusalem. On the way home his ship was wrecked in a storm and he was washed ashore on a small island called Zante. Here he became ill of a deadly fever—probably typhoid—and here he died, alone and far from family and friends. He was not quite fifty years old.

A doctor of our times, the great William Osler, has called Vesalius' book, "The greatest book ever printed, from which modern medicine dates." After four hundred years it is still a valuable work of anatomical study.

Vesalius did not, of course, clear up all questions

of human anatomy. There were many things he did not know. He made mistakes. He did not understand the circulation of the blood. But few men have contributed more in any field of knowledge than Vesalius did in those five, short, feverish years during which he and Stephan Kalkar produced their book.

Acceptance came slowly. The Galenists still occupied the university teaching positions. It took fully a hundred years for their influence to fade, and for the new anatomy of Vesalius to be allowed its proper place. But during all this time the science of anatomy was progressing.

Five years of the life of Andreas Vesalius broke through thirteen hundred years of blindness that separated him from Claudius Galen.

4

"I Dressed His Wounds—"

In the back of the barber shop the youthful apprentice was combing out the white silken strands of a gentleman's wig, mounted on a wooden head-post. He paused and looked up quickly as he heard the sound of footsteps and the opening of the front door. It was his uncle, the master barber-surgeon.

The apprentice tried not to show any trace of anxiety or excitement. With the comb and brush, he returned diligently to the task of dressing the wig.

He heard the heavy footsteps again, and in a moment he saw the polished buckled shoes and long white stockings as his uncle stood before him.

"An excellent job," the master barber-surgeon said with satisfaction. "Not an apprentice in all

Paris can dress a wig more pleasingly—and not many masters. But I have some news for you, Ambroise. Are you ready to hear what I have to say?"

Ambroise Paré could no longer conceal his excitement. He dropped the comb to the floor and let it lie there. "Yes, please!" he begged. "Tell me if the news is good or bad. What did the commissioners say?"

His uncle laughed fondly at the anxiety of his young nephew. He took off his hat and coat leisurely and loosened his collar. The summer day was very warm.

"The commissioners say the appointment as companion-surgeon at the Hotel Dieu is yours." The master sat down heavily in the big chair he used for fitting customers' wigs. "I shall miss you," he said slowly. "I shall miss you very much, Ambroise. I don't expect to find an apprentice like you again. But then, you can't remain an apprentice all your life, can you?"

Ambroise was scarcely listening. His eyes were focused on something far away. His uncle had been kind in teaching him the ways of the barber-surgeons of Paris, but Ambroise was thinking that now there would be no more combing and powdering of wigs. No more shaving of beards and cutting of hair. Or not as much, anyway.

Now, at last, he could spend most of his time in the occupation to which he knew he must dedicate his life—surgery.

The Hotel Dieu was the great charity hospital of Paris. In 1529 it was nearly nine hundred years old according to tradition. It had been founded by Saint Landry, Bishop of Paris, who established charity hospitals in each of the large cities of France. It was called the Hotel Dieu, a place for God's hospitality.

Ambroise Paré was no stranger to the hospital. He had worked there as often as possible as an apothecary boy, assisting in whatever tasks the surgeons asked of him, in addition to studying under his uncle. But now he could call himself a surgeon, for indeed he was one, the resident surgeon, who could assist the best of the master-surgeons in ministering to the sick poor of Paris.

The hospital had twelve hundred beds. More than a third of these were for single patients, which was a great luxury. Larger beds, five feet wide, were occupied by three to six patients each. There was no separation according to kinds of illness or for any other reason. A single bed might contain a man with a broken leg, a woman in childbirth, an infant with convulsions, a young man burning with fever, a middle-aged woman with tuberculosis— and a corpse that had been dead for twenty-four hours and had not yet been removed. In one section there were special beds for children—eight beds, in which lay two hundred babies and children.

Those who had beds were fortunate, however. Many patients lay on piles of straw in the large halls. The straw was seldom changed and it crawled with lice and cockroaches and other insects. There were no lights or ventilation.

One out of every five patients died. Among the surgical cases, there were almost no survivors.

On the morning of his appointment, Ambroise Paré was taken to the hospital by his uncle. In the outer hall they met two of the commissioners of the council of eight who had signed Ambroise's appointment.

The commissioners shook his hand warmly. "We welcome you in the name of God and the King, *Monsieur* Paré. We know that you will one day be one of the great surgeons of France."

Ambroise bowed humbly. "Thank you, gentlemen, for your confidence in my meager talents. I shall do my best to prove you are right."

"We are sure of that. And now, I think *Monsieur le Docteur* has more need of your services than we."

Ambroise turned to the waiting surgeon, who had come silently into the hall.

"I am glad you have come," the surgeon said. "I have been saving a case which is just right for your talents. But hurry; the man will not live an hour longer."

Ambroise shook hands with his uncle. "Goodbye, and I thank you with all my heart for your goodness and your teachings."

"Only to get myself a good apprentice," said his uncle gruffly, hiding the feelings that threatened to choke in his throat. "Make a good surgeon, now. You understand?"

Ambroise nodded silently and followed the surgeon out of the room. At the entrance to the hall of the sick he stopped and picked up a sponge from a table. He dipped the sponge in a dish of vinegar and held it before his nose as he followed the surgeon. Such was the custom, for the foulness of the air could not be endured when suddenly coming in from the outside, and the sting of the vinegar took away a little of the stench until the nostrils became accustomed to it. Each attendant practiced this upon entering the hospital in the morning.

In a dim basement hall they came upon the wretched patient. He had been lifted from his pile of straw and tied to the operating board. Ambroise Paré groaned within himself when he saw the man. A broken leg lay twisted, showing the white stumps of bone through the flesh—a compound fracture.

"You will operate," said the surgeon. "Above the knee. All is ready. Quickly now."

Other patients watched from the huddles of straw with sick, expectant eyes. Nearby, a monk fanned

the white-hot coals in a brazier and turned the cauterizing iron to heat it evenly. The knife and the saw lay beside the patient.

Ambroise Paré's heart filled with sympathy for the stricken man. "He is to die—why not let him die in peace and not torture him any more?"

"Are you to be a surgeon, or a sweeper of floors?" Ambroise's companion asked in rising anger. "Quickly, now! How else must you perfect your knowledge?"

Ambroise slowly removed his coat and let it drop to the pile of straw. Vermin scurried at the disturbance. Ambroise moved as if in a daze. He had seen and assisted at many operations, but never had he performed one alone.

The patient moaned and opened his eyes as Ambroise approached. "No—no!" he cried.

Speed was everything. A surgeon had to be fast no matter how the patient cried out. Slowing the work only increased the patient's agony.

Ambroise reached for the knife, then moved swiftly. The patient uttered a long, shrieking cry that died away as the man sank into the world of unconsciousness. Then the saw.

The surgeon was shaking his head. "Slow, slow! Three times too slow! Do you want to lose all your patients? The iron now!"

The red-hot iron filled the air with the smell of burning flesh as the tissues and blood vessels were seared over to staunch the flow of blood. Then the dressing. Ambroise quickly bound the stump of leg in strips of cloth. He stepped back at last, sweat streaming from his face. He was sure his time was less than two minutes.

"Not bad," his surgeon companion nodded more kindly and with mild approval now. "Not bad. But you will do better. And there is no need to hurry now. This man is dead."

Ambroise learned that it was a very rare thing when a surgical patient in the Hotel Dieu did not die. His heart was pained by the human misery with which he constantly lived. He yearned to do something to relieve this misery, but he did not know what to do beyond the things the barber-surgeons had taught him.

He knew that good food was as necessary for hospital patients as for anyone else, but the hospital had no regular supply of food. The nuns and monks served scanty portions that were scarcely fit to eat. For the most part, the patients had to depend on irregular contributions from the rich people of the city. The hospital doors were always open for that purpose. Anyone could bring food at any time to the patients.

Thus, for days they might starve, then suddenly they would gorge themselves on the gifts of some charitable citizen.

This was the way of the age in which he lived, and Ambroise Paré could do little to change that part of it.

Ambroise was born in 1510 near a town called Lavalle. His father was a cabinetmaker and a barber —which meant he could also do surgery. He had a brother who was a master barber-surgeon in the town of Vitré, as well as the uncle in Paris. Ambroise became interested in surgery when he was very young and studied first with his brother, then with his uncle.

Because he was poor and had little elementary schooling, Ambroise could not enter the great University of Paris. Entrance required a knowledge of Greek and Latin, and he knew neither language. For this reason, he was barred from becoming a physician. The work of a barber-surgeon, however, did not require great learning. Barber-surgeons were not of the same professional class as physicians. Rather, they were craftsmen, like bricklayers and carpenters, and surgery was combined with barbering. The man who could cut hair was qualified to amputate a leg.

Ambroise Paré knew there was far more to the art of surgery than the physicians admitted, but he was thankful that the situation permitted him to become a barber-surgeon, even though it required him to cut hair and shave whiskers.

For three years Ambroise worked and studied at the Hotel Dieu, learning all that observations of nature and his fellow surgeons could teach him there, but he wanted to learn more.

He decided to join the army. There was no regular medical corps in his day. A surgeon simply searched for the military commander or troop unit that would pay for his services and attached himself to it. So Ambroise became an army surgeon under Lieutenant-general de Montmorency in the army of Francis I, King of France. He saw his first battle service at the battle of Turin. In later years he wrote of this:

> In the year 1536 the great King Francois sent a great army to Turin to recover the cities and castles which had been taken. A great part of the army having arrived at the Pass of Suze, we found the enemy holding the passage. Captain Le Rat climbed with many soldiers from his company on a little hill. He received a shot from an arquebus in the ankle, wherewith he suddenly fell to the ground and said, "Now the Rat is taken." I dressed his wounds and God healed him.

This last sentence has become a famous quotation. It is repeated many times in the writings of Ambroise Paré. It shows the greatness of the character that was to be matched only by the greatness of the skill that Ambroise was developing. Because he could not read the ancient medical writings in Latin, he was forced to observe nature for himself. He was a pious man, a Huguenot, who gave, at every turn, credit to nature and to God for the healings he observed.

At Turin, he felt he was still learning. He wrote later, "I will tell the truth, I was not very expert at that time in matters of Chirurgery (surgery); neither was I used to dress wounds made by gunshot."

It was, in fact, his first experience with gunshot wounds. He had read that such wounds were poisoned by the gunpowder and that the only treatment was to pour boiling oil of elder into the wound. But Ambroise was thinking of the pain and suffering of the wounded men.

He wrote further, "In order not to err before using the said oil, knowing that such a thing would bring great pain to the patient, I wished to know first, how the other surgeons did for the first dressing, which was to apply said oil as hot as possible into the wound, of whom I took courage to do as they did."

But the battle of Turin produced large numbers of sorely wounded men, and Ambroise Paré's elder oil soon ran out. He had every reason to believe that if he did not use the oil the men would die of the poison of gunpowder in their wounds. Yet neither could he ignore the huge numbers of wounded pouring into the quarters he had set up.

He made the best dressing he could think of by stirring together the yolks of eggs, oil of roses, and turpentine. He applied this to the wounds and dressed them with bandages.

But he couldn't sleep that night. He worried about the poor soldiers he had been unable to treat properly. He felt sure they would lose their lives because he had failed them. At daybreak he hurried to see how the men were. He was astonished that those who had not been treated with boiling oil were feeling little pain, and that their wounds were without inflammation or swelling. They had rested well.

On the other hand, those into whose wounds he had poured the boiling oil were feverish and in agony from the pain and swelling.

"Then," Ambroise writes, "I resolved with myself

never more to burn thus cruelly poor men wounded with gunshot."

It didn't matter what the books said now; his own observations had shown him the books were dead wrong.

This sort of thing brought him into greater and greater conflict with the medical authorities of his day, and he did not hesitate to oppose them when he found he was right. When he began writing books about his observations he was attacked by the physicians of Paris as "a man without any learning" because he wrote in French instead of Latin as they did. They attacked him because his teachings did not conform to the medical practice handed down from ancient times.

But Ambroise did not flinch. To one of them he wrote, "Dare you teach me surgery, you who have never come out of your study? Surgery is learned by the eye and hand. You know nothing else but how to chatter in a chair."

For thirty years Ambroise Paré lived the hard life of an army surgeon. He served in twenty military campaigns. Between these, he returned to Paris and established private practice. He married and had children, of whom only one daughter survived.

As Ambroise grew older in years and military service his reputation grew and became known far outside military circles. In spite of the fact that he never learned Latin, he was finally admitted to the staff of the College of St. Come.

In 1559 he retired from the army and soon established a large practice among the most prominent men of France. He became surgeon to the king, and served under four different rulers. Because of his leadership, France rose to first place in the world of surgery and long remained there.

In addition to showing proper methods of treating gunshot wounds, Ambroise Paré contributed many modern surgical practices.

The method of cauterizing, or burning, had long been applied to blood vessels to stop bleeding, as well as to wounds in general. In ancient times the Greeks had tied the severed blood vessels, but this had been forgotten. Ambroise Paré rediscovered and used the method, which is called ligation. In later times, little clamps called hemostats were invented to clamp blood vessels, and these are used today in surgical operations.

Ambroise also invented artificial limbs and eyes. He introduced massage as a method of treatment. And he revived a forgotten surgical treatment for hare.ip.

Perhaps the greatest medical contribution, however, was his development of methods for aiding mothers in childbirth. In his day, it was unthinkable for a physician or surgeon to assist a mother during the delivery of her child. Such care was left to the midwives, women whose only store of knowledge was tradition and superstition. Many of them were ignorant, and they practiced a profession that was considered beneath the dignity of better people.

Ambroise Paré, whose heart had been moved to sympathy for suffering men on the battlefields of France and Italy, was also moved by the plight of mothers who suffered and oftentimes died for lack of adequate medical care during childbirth. He led the way for the invasion of medical science into the delivery room. And it was truly an invasion. In 1522 a male physician in Hamburg was burned at the stake for daring to dress as a woman and study a case of childbirth.

Ambroise showed a simple method by which an unborn child, lying in a difficult position, could be turned to the proper position before birth. This was an enormous step forward in saving the lives of babies and making childbirth easier for the mothers. In his time, a school for midwives was opened in the Hotel Dieu to replace their superstitions with medical knowledge.

Ambroise Paré died in 1590 at the age of eighty. His kindness and gentleness, and his intelligent understanding of the needs of his patients lifted surgery out of the depths of ignorance and dependence on the works of ancients, where it had lain for a dozen centuries.

Any age could be proud of a man like Ambroise Paré.

5

It Moves in a Circle!

The heart.

It beats and men live. It stops and men die. Its steady rhythm, always present, is like the motion of some separate, living thing within a man's breast. It pulses hard and wildly when he is angry, or in love, or struggling for his life. It is quiet and scarcely felt when he is content and at peace.

Is it any wonder that the heart has been the most mysterious organ of the body to men of all times?

A great physician of the sixteenth century, Fracastoro of Verona, expressed the despair—felt by physicians of his time—of ever understanding the heart. Fracastoro said, "The movements of the heart are known to God alone."

As might be expected, however, Claudius Galen had made valiant efforts to explain the function of the heart and the movement of the blood.

"There are two kinds of vessels," Galen said, as he demonstrated with the dissection of a pig. "First, are the arteries. After death, they are empty. Therefore, it is obvious that the left side of the heart, from which the arteries come, pumps air through the arteries to the different parts of the body. During life, of course, blood can be obtained from a cut artery. There is a mixture of some blood and air in them. But the important element is air.

"The veins are the other kind of vessels. You see these great veins originating in the walls of the stomach and intestine and going to the liver. Other veins go from the liver to all parts of the body. In the stomach and intestine, food is changed to *natural spirits*, which are carried by the veins to the liver. The liver, in turn, propels these *natural spirits* through other veins to all parts of the body by means of a gentle, pulsing motion similar to that of the heart.

"Within the heart, there is a wall, which divides

the heart into two parts, right and left. This wall is called the septum. Some think there is a problem as to how the blood gets from the right side to the left side of the heart. But there is really no difficulty here. Blood moves through tiny openings in the septum. It seeps through, just as sweat seeps through from the inside to the outside of the skin.

"There is no great mystery if you understand these things."

And so, since Galen had said it, this was the accepted doctrine of heart and liver function and blood flow until the time of Vesalius.

But no one who had ever had occasion to examine the heart of an animal or man had been able to find the holes Galen said were in the septum. Vesalius searched in vain for them and finally said, "I do not see how even the smallest amount of blood could pass from the right ventricle to the left through the septum."

He was unable, however, for all his great contributions to anatomy, to explain just what course the blood does follow in its movement.

There was one brilliant mind that did see part

of the solution at this time. Michael Servetus was a classmate of Vesalius in Paris when Professor Sylvius was dissecting dogs whose anatomy did not agree with Galen's theory. About 1550, Servetus wrote, "This communication (of blood) does not take place through the septum—as commonly believed, but by another admirable contrivance, the blood being transmitted through the lungs, in the course of which it is elaborated and becomes of a crimson color."

The world scarcely heard of Michael Servetus until long afterward. He was burned at the stake by John Calvin in 1553 for religious heresy.

Realdo Colombo, the student who turned against Vesalius, became a noted anatomist at Padua and in 1559 published a description of the blood flow through the lungs. It is probable that he copied it from the martyred Michael Servetus.

Against this background of error and half-truth, a sober, reserved English youth appeared at Padua in 1599 to register at the university. This youth was William Harvey of Folkstone, England.

Harvey was born in 1578, one of nine children in a pleasant and prosperous family. His brothers became merchants and traders, but William Harvey had never doubted that his own future was in medicine. He began his premedical studies at Cambridge when he was sixteen. He was twenty when he arrived at Padua.

It was like a dream come true to walk the same grounds and pass beneath the winged lion over the doors to the anatomical theater where Andreas Vesalius had walked sixty years before. The professor of anatomy was now the renowned Fabricus, who had been taught by Fallopius, who was, in turn, the student of Vesalius.

Shortly after William Harvey entered the university, Fabricus announced his own great discovery. "By most careful examination," he said, "it is possible to show that within the tubes of the veins lie tiny valves. From their structure it is obvious that as the blood forces itself against them in one direction, they open. As the blood forces against them in the other direction, they close."

William Harvey was astounded at the meaning of

this. "Then the blood cannot flow through the veins to the extremities of the body!" he exclaimed.

"Ah, we must not be too hasty," said Fabricus. "It is true that the valves close, but only partly. They slow the blood so that the tissues have time to absorb the vital spirit from the blood, and they prevent the veins from swelling as a result of too-rapid outflow of blood. Is that clear?"

Harvey nodded but remained silent. It was not clear. He did not understand it at all, but his standing in the class would suffer if he questioned the great Fabricus too much.

The question of the movement of the blood within the body took possession of Harvey's mind. At the earliest opportunity in dissection he opened a vein and examined the structure of the valves which Fabricus had found. Harvey could not believe what he saw. He nudged his companion at the dissection table.

"Look at this," he said, "and tell me if I'm wrong! See how the little valves move to open and close the vein? Imagine the blood flowing in this direction. The harder it pushes, the tighter the valves will close. The blood can't possibly flow in this direction at all! Why does Fabricus say that the valves merely slow the blood down, when they stop it entirely?"

His companion glanced around cautiously and smiled. "Who knows? But when Galen says the blood flows through the veins to the extremities of the body, would you be the first to stand up and say it does not?"

"But Fabricus—"

"Our good Fabricus is a great man. He has a noble reputation, but he remembers, too, that the mighty Vesalius was driven from the university by those who can read only Galen. He is not anxious to share that fate. And, besides, what does it matter if he alters what he sees by just a trifle to keep the wrath of Galen from his head?"

"It is not right—"

"It is very right, and I recommend you do likewise if you intend to leave Padua with a degree of Doctor of Physic in your hand."

That evening, in the dim twilight of his room, Harvey stood by the cloth windows awkwardly tying a rag about his left arm, above the elbow.

His roommate, John, of Cambridge, stared at the strange procedure. "What in the world are you trying to do?" he asked.

"Come and help me," said Harvey. "Here—take the ends of this and tie them for me. No, a little tighter—just a little."

John obliged. Harvey clenched his fist about a small stick. "See?" he said, pointing to his arm. "The veins stand out, gorged with blood because the flow is restricted—but not cut off—by the tourniquet. And see these?"

"See what?"

"These little swellings on the veins. Each one marks the location of a valve. Now, I can prove which way the blood is flowing in the vein."

"Listen," said John. "I know which way Galen says it flows. That's all I want to know."

Harvey ignored his words. "Look. I press my thumb on the vein at a point in my forearm and stop the flow of blood completely. Now you press your finger upward along the vein so as to force the blood past the tourniquet."

John obeyed. "So what does that prove?" he

asked doubtfully, unwilling to accept any new ideas.

"Observe that the swelling of the vein is gone," said Harvey. "You have forced the blood upward beyond the restriction. The valves keep it from returning. Now, if Galen and Fabricus are right, the vein should swell again as the blood fills it. But blood cannot fill it as long as my finger stops the blood from moving higher than my forearm. The blood does not flow *down* my arm to fill the vein because the valves hold it back. But now I release my finger and the blood does flow *up* the vein in my arm."

John stared as the vein on Harvey's arm slowly swelled again. Then, triumphantly, Harvey untied the rag and threw it across the room.

"You see," he exclaimed, "blood does not flow outward in the veins! Not at all! It flows only inward from the extremities toward the body. Galen was wrong, and our good Professor Fabricus knows it and is quite afraid to admit it!"

"You'll get yourself thrown out before your first year is up. Vesalius himself didn't last very long after he published—and heaven knows you're no

Vesalius," John concluded with a shake of his head.

"I'm afraid you're right there," said Harvey quietly. "But there's something about the blood that none of them knows, and someday I'm going to find out the truth about it!"

Each group of students from the various countries of the world elected leaders of their particular "nation." William Harvey led the large group of English students at Padua during his stay. He was active in their society; he endured with them the miserable living conditions of the dormitories—the poor and inadequate supply of food, the rough beds, and the cloth windows that did not keep out the wind and winter cold.

He graduated from Padua in 1602, with the degree of Doctor of Physic.

Further studies at Cambridge brought him the degree of Doctor of Medicine in 1604. He joined the official organization of doctors, the College of Physicians, and set up practice in London. He was on his way to becoming a prosperous and successful physician.

It was not enough.

The mysteries that had haunted him since those student days at Padua would not let him alone. He was going to find the answer to the puzzle of blood movement, no matter what else he did.

The valves in the veins were the clue, he thought. Later studies and dissections had shown him that the valves were certainly not for the purpose of keeping the blood from falling to the extremities of the arms and legs because of gravity, as some said. There were valves in the veins of the neck, too, and they kept the blood from flowing *up*. There was a pattern to it all. Everywhere in the body the valves kept blood from flowing in the veins away from the heart. They permitted a flow only toward the heart.

This being so, the idea which was older than Hippocrates—that the blood moved in a pulsing, back-and-forth motion—this idea could not be true. The blood flowed in one direction only. In the arteries it flowed away from the heart. In the veins it flowed toward the heart. Did this mean it flowed in a circle, from the heart out to the extremities and back again? What else could it mean?

And what did the heart itself do?

The heart is divided vertically by the septum into two sections which anatomists call the right heart and the left heart. Harvey had long since concluded, as Vesalius had, that the idea of holes in the septum was utter nonsense. The septum was an impenetrable wall. Yet blood did go somehow from the right heart to the left heart.

Each side of the heart is further divided into two chambers, which are separated by a partition containing a valve that allows a flow of blood only from the upper chamber to the lower chamber. The upper chambers are called the auricles; the lower chambers are called the ventricles.

Harvey did not know of the work of Servetus, but his studies led to the same conclusions reached by the martyred physician. He saw that the blood poured into the right auricle from the large veins leading from the stomach and liver and from the extremities of the body. This blood passed into the right ventricle and from there it was propelled to the lungs. But a large vein from the lungs poured blood into the left auricle of the heart.

Could there by any question that this was the same blood, even though it was dark when it left the heart and bright when it returned? Harvey was convinced there was not. The lungs did something to change the color, but it was the same blood.

So he had a continuous circuit. The blood passed from the right side of the heart to the lungs, and *through* them to the left side of the heart. There was no need for invisible holes in the septum! Here was a complete path around a circle, in which the right heart served as a pump to pass blood from the large veins of the body through the lungs and back to the left heart.

How simple when it was finally understood! Galen had been right about that point, at least.

And then the full picture became apparent. The heart was not just a simple pump. The heart was two complete and separate pumps; there were two separate circuits in the body, around which the blood flowed.

After leaving the lungs and entering the left auricle, the blood passed to the left ventricle, from which it was forced through the large aorta and distributed to the arteries throughout the body.

Harvey concluded that the blood was discharged from the arteries into the tiny particles of the flesh and was then drawn back into the veins to make its way back to the heart, the lungs, and the heart again, then once more through the arteries. Each time, he saw, it was refreshed by its passage through the lungs, and waste material was removed from it.

The ancient teachings had said that the blood was used up at the end of its travel and was constantly being formed anew from the food taken in. This didn't seem likely now, since there was obviously a return flow of blood from all portions of the body. Harvey considered the question: How much blood does the heart pump, anyway?

He measured the capacity of a ventricle of the heart. It held about two ounces. The average rate of heart beat was about seventy-two per minute. If the ventricle was completely emptied at each beat, the total amount of blood pumped in an hour would be three times the weight of a man!

Harvey conservatively supposed that only an

eighth of the blood in a ventricle might be ejected at each beat—although it is actually much more. But even so, the quantity of blood pumped by the heart was enormous. Where did such an amount of blood come from?

Again, there could be only one answer. It was not used up at the end of its travel and reformed from the food in the stomach. Such a thing was mathematically impossible. The blood had to circulate. The same blood was pumped endlessly around the circuit of veins, heart, lungs, and arteries.

Harvey did not mention his studies and his proofs

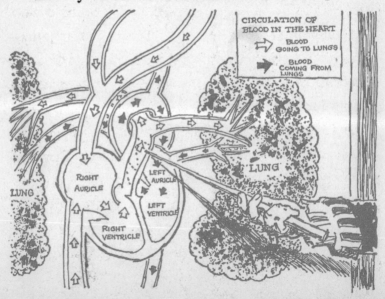

CIRCULATION OF
BLOOD IN THE HEART

⇨ BLOOD GOING TO LUNGS

➡ BLOOD COMING FROM LUNGS

LUNG

RIGHT AURICLE

LEFT AURICLE

LEFT VENTRICLE

RIGHT VENTRICLE

LUNG

until fourteen years after leaving Padua. Then he spoke of them only to a small group of students to whom he lectured in 1616. He said at that time, "It is proved by the structure of the heart that the blood is perpetually transferred through the lungs into the aorta, as by two clacks of a water bellows to raise water. It is proved by the ligature that there is a transit of blood from the arteries to the veins; whereby it is demonstrated that the perpetual movement of the blood in a circle is brought about by the beat of the heart."

His conclusions were firmly in his mind at this time, but he was still cautious. He studied and experimented for twelve more years before announcing his discovery to the world. During this time he became prosperous. He was appointed physician to King James I. He was elected to a high position in the College of Physicians in which he supervised physicians of the city in their practice. Then, in 1628, after more than twenty years of study and experiment, he published his work to the world.

Here he stated boldly for physicians of every nation to read, " . . . the blood passes through the lungs and heart by action of the ventricles, and is sent for distribution to all parts of the body, where it makes its way into the veins and pores of the flesh, and then flows by the veins . . . into the vena cava and right auricle of the heart, and this in such quantity . . . as cannot possibly be supplied by the (food), and is much greater than can be required for mere purposes of nutrition; it is absolutely necessary to conclude that the blood in the animal body is impelled in a circle, and is in a state of ceaseless motion; that this is the act or function which the heart performs by means of its pulse; and that it is the sole and only end of the motion and contraction of the heart."

These facts are so common to our thinking today that it is very difficult to realize what an upheaval they represented in the thinking of Harvey's day.

As it had been with Vesalius, so with Harvey; the publication of the great book on circulation brought a storm of violence and abuse. Harvey's medical practice dwindled as rival physicians denounced him as a crackpot. His work of twenty years was attacked in a vicious book written in two weeks by a Scottish physician living in France. Another accused him of creating a medical scandal by trying to tear down so many tried and true and beautiful medical explanations. The most violent of all continued to maintain that if Galen's descriptions did not fit modern dissections, it was because nature had changed and no one should accuse Galen of error. In Paris, his theory was called "paradoxical, useless, false, impossible, absurd, and harmful."

But slowly, one by one, supporters began to come over to Harvey's side as evidence for his theory accumulated. He had the rare privilege of living long enough to see his revolutionary discoveries generally accepted by the leading medical men of his time.

Harvey's greatness lies not merely in his momentous discovery of the circulation of the blood. It lies equally in his method of discovery, a genuinely scientific method. He made observations, he proposed theories to explain the observations, and he devised experiments to test theories. This scientific method of discovery was as important to the world as was his announcement of the circulation of the blood.

His book stands beside that of Vesalius. Upon these two, modern medicine is founded.

For all his great work, very little is known of the personal life of William Harvey. He lived through a time of great civil war in England. He was the personal physician of James I, and the physician and close friend of Charles I, who was executed at the end of the civil war. In all the turbulence about him, Harvey pursued a serene, steadfast course that seemed undisturbed by war or personal misfortune. He lived in an age of great men. He was a young man when Shakespeare died. He must have met Galileo, who was teaching at Padua when Harvey was a student there. He probably met Milton, the poet, in Italy.

William Harvey died in 1657 at the age of eighty. He was truly one of the world's great discoverers.

6

The World Unseen

Through the dark streets of the university town of Bologna, Italy, Professor Marcello Malpighi moved wearily. He would have to cease working these late hours at the university, he thought, or else stand the extravagance of taking a carriage home. He was so very tired. But he had just turned sixty-one. A man of that age had some right to be tired, he supposed.

He didn't want to be tired, and he didn't want to be old. He really didn't feel old. Not inside, anyway. There was so much yet to see in the fairyland he had discovered. If only the world around him were not so full of enemies and fools. If only they would let him alone. That was not asking too much, was it? Just to be let alone to practice medicine, to study, to learn, to dream, and explore this fairyland.

He turned the corner of the dusty, rutted street and came in sight of his own small villa, relieved that he had only a short way yet to go this night. Then his heart leaped in sudden fright, and he stumbled in a deep rut and fell to his knees.

But his eyes held to the sight that made him sick with fear. A small light, a dancing flame, moved in the distance. He was certain it was at his own villa. A fire!

He rose painfully to his feet. Stumbling in the darkness, he ran heavily onward. Every step proved his first fear was right. The fire was at his own place. But as he neared, he saw it was not the house that was burning, but something in the yard beside the house. A figure—no, two figures—moved silently against the flames.

Malpighi approached the house and let himself in through a side door. He stopped and groaned in agony. A lighted lamp stood on a sideboard near the door. In its glow he saw utter ruin.

The furniture was broken and overturned. The

draperies were torn and the floor slashed. He grasped the lamp and ran to his workroom. Here, all his cabinets were broken open. His precious specimens were strewn and smashed on the floor. But worst of all, his instruments were shattered beyond recognition. He set the lamp down and leaned weakly against the door. Who had done this to him? Why?

A sharp sound from behind caused him to whirl about. But not fast enough. He had a momentary glimpse of a figure in a black mask and cape. A splintered chair leg was raised above his head. It crashed down upon him in a flood of agony.

His upraised arm caught part of the blow, which would have otherwise crushed his skull. He dropped to the floor, sick with pain, but consciousness remained.

He sensed a second figure behind the first, and heard a voice. "You've got to finish him now. Here, let me."

Malpighi heard the snick of a dagger withdrawn from its scabbard.

"No!" the other figure said. "This is enough. Look around and see if there's anything we've missed. Then let's get out of here."

Malpighi looked up blindly in the direction of the voices. The voices! He knew them. There could be no doubt.

"Why?" he uttered hoarsely. "Why have you done this? My instruments—my work—who have I harmed—?"

One of the figures laughed thickly. "Because you are a fool, and we are tired of fools. I think the world will be plagued with no more of your nonsense from now on."

"Kill him!" the other figure whispered fiercely. "We can't leave him—"

"There's nothing to fear. He's had lesson enough to inspire others of his kind. Let's be gone."

Malpighi heard their departing steps. Against the wall he saw the dying flicker of the flames in his yard, the flames that had consumed his papers, his books. . . .

His masked assailants—he could call their names. They were two of the professors at the university. But who would be convinced that respected university professors had attacked him like

common thieves and murderers?

No one.

He sank to the floor and his pain and grief were released in the sobs that shook him, and in the tears that flowed from his eyes.

A lifetime of work, and a message of beauty and wonder to give to the world—and this was the world's reward.

Marcello Malpighi was born near Bologna in 1628. When he graduated from medical school he wrote his thesis on the subject of Hippocrates and the superiority of his teachings for physicians. Malpighi was a gentle man and he admired the teachings of Hippocrates that appealed for a humanitarian approach to the sick.

Malpighi did not plan to spend his life in the practice of medicine, however. He saw the world of living things as a frontier that had scarcely been explored. He intended to devote his life to such exploration.

At the age of twenty-eight he became a professor at the University of Pisa.

One day, someone whose name we do not know told Malpighi of a strange and wonderful new device.

"I want you to see this machine," the man said. "You put your eye to it and suddenly you see things that were before too utterly small for your eye to behold!"

"I have heard of them," said Malpighi. "They come from Holland, where they are called flea glasses because they make a flea appear as big as a dog. They are only toys."

"Not this device I am speaking of. True, it does make things appear bigger, but far more wonderfully than the flea glasses ever did. This is an improvement that was made by Galileo Galilei some time before his death. I have just seen one for the first time. You must look for yourself."

"I have no time for toys," said Malpighi, "but I will look because you insist."

In the room of his friend, Malpighi looked through the small tube at a sight that was stranger and more marvelous than anything he had ever seen in all his previous investigations.

"What in the world is this?" he asked.

"The scale of a fish. Try this now—this is a piece of tissue from an unhatched chick. I hold it up and you see nothing but whitish skin. But under the microscope. . . ."

Malpighi looked again. He looked for a long time at the lacelike pattern before him. Flesh was solid, he had been taught. There were no smaller parts to it. Now he saw a fairyland of exquisite structure that had been hidden in the piece of chick tissue.

He straightened finally and breathed a long sigh. "I must have one of these!" he said. "I must have one immediately, no matter what the cost!"

As it turned out, the cost was enormously high: his peace of mind and soul for the rest of his life.

He became possessed by the wonderland of tiny structures revealed in solid tissue by the lens. No anatomist had ever dreamed that flesh was anything but solid substance. But everything Malpighi put under his lens seemed to be constructed of tiny building blocks as delicate as lace, as exquisite as fairyland. The opening of this world was almost overwhelming. Malpighi was like a child suddenly in a wonderland which was greater than his senses could ever encompass.

After his first wild burst of enthusiasm, Malpighi set out upon a course of orderly study and discovery. The tissues of larger animals and man were of such complexity that he knew it would be simpler to start with the small things first. Insects, smaller animals, plant tissue.

The silkworm was an object of great importance at this time because of the silk industry in Europe. Malpighi turned his lens on the silkworm and prepared an elaborate study of its anatomy. He published two large volumes on plant anatomy, as he called it. Then he turned to the frog, and came upon one of his most momentous discoveries.

To the naked eye the lung of the frog looks like nothing more than a pale membrane, so thin that light can be seen through it. Malpighi arranged a dissection so that the lung of a living frog could be seen with the microscope. Here he witnessed a miraculous sight, one that William Harvey would have given much to see.

Harvey had said that arteries simply branch into smaller and smaller vessels until they finally pour the blood into spaces in the tissue, where it distributes nourishment and is then gathered up by the veins for return to the heart and lungs. He believed correctly that the arteries joined with the veins to make a complete circle, but he never knew exactly how this was done.

Malpighi found out. In the lung of a frog he saw the tiny branches of the arteries that became as fine as hair, and he saw that they continued on and on. Nowhere did they empty the blood into small cavities in the tissues. He followed them to their limits and saw that they began to regroup into larger channels—the veins. And he saw the living blood flow through these hairlike channels.

He wrote of it, "I saw the blood, showered down in tiny streams through the arteries, after the fashion of a flood."

He had seen the capillaries, the connecting link between arteries and veins, the final link in the circulatory system, which Harvey had never found. Now, the circle was complete.

Malpighi said of the capillaries, ". . . these vessels . . . proceed on this side from the vein and on the other from the artery . . . . Hence it was clear . . . that the blood flowed along sinuous vessels and was not poured into spaces, but was always contained within tubules, and that its dispersion is due to the multiple winding of the vessels."

He had returned to Bologna by this time, and here, in 1661, when he was thirty-three years old, he published his discovery of the capillaries. Four years later he wrote of his discovery of the corpuscles.

There is no more tragic example of the hostility and hatred with which the world greets new ideas that conflict with the old than the life of Marcello Malpighi. After his publications began to appear, he was hounded and driven without ceasing for the rest of his life. His fellow professors at Bologna ridiculed his announcements viciously.

Malpighi fled from Bologna to the University of Messina, where he taught for four years. He continued his studies of microscopic anatomy. He examined the human liver and wrote a treatise on it. He studied the skin and wrote of it. One layer of skin is called by his name to this day. He studied the spleen, and one of its structures is today called the Malpighian corpuscle.

With this work, Malpighi founded the science of anatomy of the tissues. Later generations were to regard him as the greatest anatomist of all time excepting only Vesalius. But few of his contemporaries regarded him with anything but scorn.

He was driven from Messina by the attacks on his work and he returned to Bologna, but his colleagues would allow him no peace anywhere in the professional world. He continued to study and publish his findings, and his enemies continued to torment him.

One of the greatest mysteries of all time was, of course, the generation of new life. The ancients had generally believed that the development of new life within the womb or within an egg was simply a process of growing bigger, that the creature was always completely formed, but merely of a different size.

Malpighi devised an important series of experiments which involved the opening of chicken eggs at intervals of six hours during the early stages of their incubation. He applied the microscope to the tiny cloud within the egg that represented the beginning of life. Here again, the view was almost as wonderful and as startling as his first view of blood flowing through the capillaries of the frog.

He wrote, for all the world to know, including his blind enemies who would not consider the evidence of the microscope, "The heart of the chicken begins as a tiny tube. It coils on itself and seems to spin out of itself a heart and a set of blood vessels. The spinal cord and the brain begin as a groove in the back of the creature. The eyes start from tiny specks that grow into small blisters."

Marcello Malpighi was truly on the edge of a new world. But in his own land it was as if all other men were blind.

The torment of his enemies was climaxed by the attack on his life and property by two of his fellow professors at the University of Bologna when he was sixty-one years old. It was more than he could endure. Soon after the attack he received an invitation to come to Rome as personal physician to Pope

Innocent XII, who was one of the few who had a high regard for his work.

Malpighi eagerly accepted the opportunity to receive the safety and security of the Vatican. His life became happier and more peaceful than it had ever been. But there was little time for scientific work. His microscopes and his fairyland of living tissues were put away. There was little time, too, for him to enjoy his new-found peace. He died in Rome in 1694 at the age of sixty-six, a martyr to the ignorance and stupidity that had surrounded him.

During the same time Marcello Malpighi was making his momentous discoveries, an amateur scientist in Holland was making great strides in discovering the world of the small. This was Anton van Leeuwenhoek, who was four years younger than Malpighi. He was not a professional scientist. Rather, he was in the drapery business, and he made microscopes as a hobby.

The Dutch had been early masters of lens grinding. From their experience in making spectacles had grown the early flea glasses of about 1590. These had a magnifying power of perhaps ten diameters. But van Leeuwenhoek, who made approximately two hundred microscopes in his lifetime, was a master lens maker and obtained magnifications of almost two hundred diameters with his simple lenses.

Leeuwenhoek was able to confirm Malpighi's observation of capillary circulation. He did it in the tail of a tadpole and described it in a letter, as he did most of his discoveries.

"Upon examining the tail of this creature," he wrote, "a sight presented itself more delightful than any my eyes had ever beheld; for here I discovered more than fifty circulations of the blood, in different places, while the animal lay quiet in water, and I could bring it before the microscope to my wish. For I saw, not only that the blood in many places was conveyed through exceedingly minute vessels from the middle of the tail towards the edges, but that each of these vessels had a curve or turning, and carried the blood back towards the middle of the tail in order to be conveyed to the heart. Here, it plainly appeared to me that the blood vessels I now saw in the animal and which bear the names of arteries and veins, are, in fact, one and the same, that they are properly termed arteries so long as they convey the blood to the farthest extremities of its vessels, and veins when they bring it back to the heart."

This was quite a magnificent observation for a man who sold draperies by day and ground lenses for his own microscopes by night! Leeuwenhoek was entirely self-taught. He had no university education nor any knowledge of Greek or Latin or the classical texts which were written in these languages. But he

had a tremendous skill in grinding lenses, which made his instruments far better than most. And with this skill was combined a capacity for alert observation and intelligent reporting. He wrote letters telling of his discoveries to the Royal Society of London and sent them drawings of blood corpuscles and spermatozoa. He described for the first time the important striations of the muscle fibers.

The most important of his discoveries, however, was that of bacteria and protozoa, the microscopic plant and animal forms, some of which cause disease and some of which are of great benefit to man.

This discovery came about in a quite simple manner. He scraped moisture from his own teeth and looked at it through his lens. He was startled to find, as he described it, ". . . little animals, more numerous than all the people in the Netherlands, and moving about in the most delightful manner!"

Leeuwenhoek was delighted, but not many other people were. His countrymen and scientists everywhere cried angrily, "Who has little animals crawling around on their teeth?"

He came in for his share of opposition, but it did

not approach the inhumanity that Malpighi suffered. He answered his critics rather mildly. "I will be so bold to say, these gentlemen . . . have not attained to a degree of proficiency to observe such objects truly. I not only behold their motions in all directions, but I see them turn about, remain still, and sometimes expire; and the larger kinds of them I see as plainly running along as we do with the naked eye. Nay, I see some of them open their mouths, and move the organs of parts within them; and I have discovered hairs at the mouth of some of these species though they were some thousand degrees less than a grain of sand."

The horizons of knowledge were expanding, even though the countrymen of Anton van Leewenhoek did not like his realistic descriptions of the "little animals" running around on their teeth!

7

The Milkmaid and the Plague

Constantinople in the year 1716 was not the safest place in the world to bring a wife and young son. But when Edward Wortley Montagu was appointed British Ambassador to Turkey in that year neither he nor the Lady Mary Wortley Montagu thought for a moment that she should stay behind. Both were adventurers, and the thought of Oriental life stirred them with excitement. They gave no more than passing thought to the dangers of political unrest, assassins, and the various dread diseases of the Orient.

A few months later Lady Mary had her most exciting expectations fulfilled. They were invited to the strangest party in the world, a smallpox party.

The Montagus were cultured and wealthy, and they made friends among the most influential Turks. It was the home of one of these that the ambassador and his lady entered that fall evening in 1716.

"You do my humble house an honor," said their Turkish host as they entered.

"It is we who are honored," said the ambassador. "Your gardens are magnificent."

Their host bowed again. From inside the house came the rich aroma of Turkish foods, rare even yet to the English appetite. The party was small; no more than two dozen were present, and they were all close members of the family except the Ambassador and Lady Montagu.

When their meal was finished, their host led them to the adjoining room, where they took chairs in an open circle. "It is time for the ingrafting woman," he said. "Let her attend."

Lady Mary Montagu gave an involuntary start at the sight of an old woman who was ushered into the room. Poorly dressed, and far from tidy, she contrasted with the wealthy, fashionable Turks who awaited her coming with anticipation.

"You first, sir?" she croaked to the host.

He waved to the ambassador. "My guests to begin with."

Lord Montagu hastily shook his head. "We wish but to watch, though not to disown your great kindness."

"You are cautious." Their host smiled. "But our ways must seem strange in many things. My nephew, then," he said to the old woman and gestured to the young man next to the ambassador.

The old crone approached slowly. She touched the young man's arm. "Which vein, sir?"

"Does it matter?"

"No, but you must choose."

"Here, then." The young man touched a pale vein in his extended arm.

The woman withdrew a long, coarse needle from the depths of her clothing. With a swift motion, she scratched deeply and drew blood. Then she withdrew a nutshell from inside her clothing, next to her skin, where the shell had been kept at body temperature.

Lady Mary knew what was in that nutshell. It

was matter—pus—from the open pustule of a smallpox victim. She could not help a slight shudder as the old woman dipped the needle into the substance and withdrew it with the tip covered. This she pressed into the wound in the young man's arm. Then she dressed the wound by binding a hollow bit of shell over it. She moved on to the next person.

In the days that followed this strange event, Lady Mary Montagu kept in close touch with the family of her Turkish host, anxious to know the results of this procedure the Turks called ingrafting. It was supposed to make them immune to the dread smallpox. It looked as if it should give them the disease, instead!

One by one, the guests who had been ingrafted became ill as if with mild smallpox, some more seriously than others. But at the end of a month all were revived, and none had died of the illness. Lady Mary was introduced to Turks who had been ingrafted many years before and who had gone through the severest kind of smallpox epidemics without contracting the disease. She was convinced that here was a kind of Oriental miracle.

To her friends in England she wrote, "I am going to tell you a thing that will make you wish yourself here. The smallpox, so fatal, and so general amongst us, is here entirely harmless, by the invention of ingrafting, which is the term they give it. There is a set of old women who make it their business to perform the operation, every autumn, in the month of September, when the great heat is abated.

"There is no example of anyone who has died of it, and you may believe I am very well satisfied of the safety of the experiment since I intend to try it on my dear little son. I am patriotic enough to take pains to bring this useful invention into fashion in England."

In March of 1717 young Edward Wortley Montagu, Jr. was ingrafted. He not only survived, but became immune to smallpox, just as the Turks promised.

Upon the return of the Montagus to England in 1718 Lady Mary did indeed take pains to bring ingrafting into fashion. Like a whirlwind, she carried the news of it everywhere she went. She urged her friend, the Princess of Wales, to have the chil-

dren of the royal family treated. There was great
hesitancy to risk the royal children, so experiments
were carried out on seven condemned criminals who
were offered pardons in exchange for their participa-
tion. Six orphan children were also treated. Afterward, all of these were exposed to smallpox, but all
proved immune. The young princes were then
ingrafted.

This great innovation soon spread throughout
England and to Europe. It was called variolation
by the English, and centers of inoculation were set
up with medical specialists to do the work.

Smallpox is almost unknown in the civilized
countries of the world today, but until very recent
times it was one of the world's greatest scourges.
Millions died of it, and other millions were dis-
figured and maimed. In the year when variolation
was introduced in England, there was a smallpox
death rate of four thousand per year per million of
population. In later years, in Germany, for example,
where control measures were strictly enforced, the
death rate became only three per year per million
of population. In the London Asylum for the Blind,

two thirds of the inmates had been blinded by small-pox.

It was no wonder that the news of this strange, half-frightening Oriental practice was greeted with joy.

Variolation, however, held many dangers. The process was not easily controlled. In some cases the reaction was mild enough, but in others a full-blown case of smallpox resulted and sometimes caused death. The smallpox resulting from variolation, whether mild or severe, was highly contagious. Often, a single person who had been treated became the center of a raging epidemic in his locality as others caught the disease from him.

For all these reasons variolation was approached with hesitation and was rejected by many. It was a subject of stormy debate for many decades. It was, however, a step in the right direction. But the final answer was yet to come. Three quarters of a century were to pass before it arrived.

One day in 1762 a country boy of thirteen, who was the son of the Vicar of Berkeley in Gloucestershire, England, was apprenticed to a Dr. Ludlow in a nearby village. The boy was Edward Jenner, and the only thing he had ever wanted to do in his young life was to study living, growing things and to become a doctor.

For seven years he served Dr. Ludlow and learned all he could of the elements of medicine and the preparation of herbs and drugs. Smallpox was often mentioned in the doctor's office.

A young woman patient once spoke lightly of it and laughed at Dr. Ludlow's concern about a case of smallpox to which she had been exposed. She had not been inoculated.

"I don't have to worry," the young woman said. "And I certainly wouldn't endure the torture of inoculation. You see, I won't ever get smallpox. I've had the cowpox, and anybody who's had cowpox can never get smallpox. See?"

She extended her arms to show Dr. Ludlow the faint scars left by cowpox.

The doctor smiled. "I have heard of this tradition of the country folk, and I only hope you are right," he said. "But I wouldn't put too much confidence in it. Be safe, and stay as far from small-pox as you can."

Young Edward Jenner heard the young woman's remarks and they stayed with him all through the remaining years of his apprenticeship with Dr. Lud-low and through the two years of formal medical training with the great Dr. John Hunter in London.

Edward spoke of it on occasion to Dr. Hunter. "What if there is some truth to this story of the milkmaids back in Gloucester, that an attack of cowpox makes them immune to smallpox?"

"Well, what if there is?" asked Dr. Hunter.

"Do you suppose . . .? Well, what if it were pos-sible to deliberately give a person cowpox—which would not make him very sick—and by that means make him immune to smallpox? Would it not be worth taking a mild cowpox if it meant no more danger from smallpox?"

Dr. Hunter's thin face was severe and intense. "Look about you: the blind, the crippled, the dead —all over London, all over England and Europe. The world would be willing to take more than a small risk to escape the plague of smallpox. I do not know if your thought has any value or not. But I say, find out!"

Dr. Hunter tried to get Edward Jenner to remain in London and practice medicine, but Edward hated the ugliness of the great city with its factory smoke and stench of sewage. He longed for the open countryside, and he hurried there as fast as he could when his training was over. Dr. Hunter was disappointed, but they remained close friends and corresponded much during the remainder of Dr. Hunter's lifetime.

In Berkeley, Dr. Edward Jenner began the routine of a country village doctor. His old friends were glad to have him back, and he prospered. For seven years, until 1778, he gave all his attention to his medical practice. Then, in that year, a smallpox epidemic struck Berkeley and the surrounding villages. Life in them came almost to a standstill as the shadow of the plague spread over the land.

Edward remembered again the dream he had once had, in what now seemed so long ago, the dream of conquering the great killer. But there was nothing to be done now; it was upon them. He had to treat the smallpox victims as best he knew how —which meant trying to keep them comfortable, and hoping they lived. Many of them however, prayed for death rather than life, if they were to be scarred and maimed by the disease.

Inoculations were available at stations which the doctors set up throughout the valley. Edward had little faith in variolation; he had seen too many disasters resulting from it. And he remembered his own childhood agony when he had been forced to submit to it. But he gave it to those who requested it.

One family of dairy farmers—most of the valley's inhabitants were engaged in dairying—came to him for inoculation, but three of the milk hands said confidently, "We don't need it. We just want to be on the safe side."

"And why don't you need it?" asked Edward Jenner impatiently. "If you've been inoculated previously let's not waste time."

"No, we want it," they said hastily. "But we've had cowpox, you see, so we wouldn't get the smallpox anyway."

There it was again, Edward thought. Why hadn't

he done something about it before now? But it wasn't entirely too late.

"Eight days from now," he said to the milk hands, "you should experience a slight fever and a few pustules. If you are truly immune, however, this won't happen. Will you come to me on the eighth day and let me see for myself?"

They promised, and Edward saw that of all he had inoculated these three were the only ones who did not have the usual reaction.

Was there truth in the old tradition, after all?

If so, how did this thing work, anyway?

He began scouring the countryside and making records of those who said they'd had cowpox. He noted whether or not they had taken smallpox and if they could react to inoculation. This work stretched into months and years, long after the epidemic was over. The evidence began to accumulate. Edward spoke of it in the local medical societies to which he belonged, until his fellow physicians told him to stop wearying them with the subject.

Then the carefully built-up evidence seemed to

fall apart. There were cases of those who had experienced cowpox but had later taken smallpox as well. There seemed to be no doubt of this. As the records grew, there was a steady proportion who seemed not to have been made immune by the cowpox.

And finally, after long search—it was almost five years—he recognized the very simple answer to this problem. Any kind of inflammation of the cows which the dairy hands acquired was called cowpox. But not all such inflammation was cowpox. Several different diseases were involved here. And *one* of them, which was true cowpox, was capable of conferring the precious immunity to smallpox.

Additional years passed without very much work on immunization, because Edward's growing practice—the largest in the valley—took all his time, and the work of identifying the true cowpox and separating it from the false cowpox went slowly.

At last he had it, however, and then he discovered another drawback. The milkers who got cowpox from the cows were immune from smallpox only if they contracted cowpox at the height of the cow's illness. This was another puzzle that took Edward long months to untangle.

Finally, Edward was taken ill himself, with typhus fever. It cost him another year—and almost took his life.

It was 1796, almost twenty years after beginning his study, before he was convinced he knew the answers. True cowpox, taken at the proper time, would confer immunity from smallpox.

Now, it had to be proved to the whole world!

In that year of 1796 a young milkmaid named Sarah Nelmes came to see Edward. Her hands were swollen and bandaged to cover the ugly red pustules of the cowpox.

"I don't know why I'm here," she said pertly. "I'm not sick. All of us milkmaids expect to get the cow-pox sooner or later. There's nothing to worry about, but they made me come to see you. It is going to be all right, isn't it?" she added now with a trace of anxiety.

Edward had been staring intently at the sores on her hands. "Yes—yes, of course it's going to be all right," he said. "And what's more, you are very fortunate that you will not ever be in any danger of smallpox the rest of your life."

He dressed the sores. "You must come again tomorrow afternoon. I will be expecting you."

For a long time after Sarah Nelmes had gone, Edward Jenner sat quietly in his study. The time had come. He knew what he must do. He knew that in the back of his mind he had already chosen the next person who must help him. But he didn't know how he was going to do the necessary persuading.

That evening he rode to the other side of the village to the cottage of the Phipps family. He sat down in the kitchen of gardener Phipps and his wife and explained about his work—much of which they already knew from the years of gossip about it in the village.

"I need the help now of someone to whom I can give an inoculation of cowpox from a human being and whom I can later inoculate with smallpox to prove he is immune. This must be someone who has not previously been inoculated or had cowpox or smallpox."

Mrs. Phipps smiled. "We can't help you, Doctor.

Both of us have been inoculated."

"I know," said Edward hesitantly. "I was thinking of young James." He nodded toward the eight-year-old boy playing on the other side of the room.

Edward Jenner survived the resulting explosion from Mrs. Phipps and the cold anger of gardener Phipps. He explained patiently once again and assured them the danger was slight. He pictured to them his hope of a world free of the dread plague.

It was Mr. Phipps who began to be persuaded at last. After hours of discussion, he said wearily, "I believe in you, Dr. Jenner. You may have James for the test."

It was May 14, 1796.

Sarah Nelmes had kept her appointment, and now she was told what the doctor intended to do. She didn't like it. This was not the kind of thing ordinary doctors did. She wished she had never come.

Edward Jenner knew he had to hurry, before everyone in the room changed his mind and ran out. Quickly, he opened one of the most inflamed pustules on Sarah's hand. James Phipps whimpered in fright.

"Just a tiny scratch," said Edward to the boy. "That's all there will be. . . ."

Quickly he acted. The boy cried out, more from fear than pain. Mrs. Phipps had to be restrained by her husband. Once more. Then it was over.

"There will be a little fever for a few days and a few cowpox pustules," said Edward. "He will not be gravely ill."

His predictions came true exactly as he said. But the big test remained. The first of July was the date chosen for inoculation with smallpox matter.

Edward couldn't restrain his own uneasiness as the day approached. But he knew he had to go ahead. This was no different from an ordinary variolation. It was just that if anything went wrong—well, he was the one responsible. It was he who had persuaded the Phippses that no harm would come to their child.

The Phippses kept their appointment. Young James was no longer afraid. It was Edward now who trembled as he applied pus from a smallpox sore to a scratch on the boy's arm.

Then eight days of waiting to learn whether he

had brought death or life.

If the boy were not immune he would develop the signs of smallpox in eight days. If it had been a particularly virulent strain of smallpox. . . .

Edward refused to let his mind dwell on the negative possibilities.

Eight days. They were the longest Edward Jenner ever knew. He visited James Phipps every day. But on the eighth day no sign of inflammation appeared. On the twelfth day James Phipps was still healthy and active and his skin was clear. Then Edward knew he had reached the end of his long quest. In his hands lay the means to conquer the killer smallpox.

During the following year other inoculations were made, and Edward wrote up the history of twenty-three of these in a paper to the Royal Society of London.

The meat was too strong for the Society's stomachs. They immediately rejected the paper, refusing to have anything to do with something as fantastic as immunization by means of matter taken originally from cows.

Edward was persuaded to publish the report independently, which he did. Thus the news of the great discovery was distributed to all the world. As usual, it was attacked bitterly by some and received well by others. Physicians tried it. Some made tragic mistakes, which nearly destroyed the use of it. Others, following Edward Jenner's instructions closely, were successful.

In France his method was ridiculed at first with the name "vaccination," which means "en-cowing." The name stuck, however, and became respectable, and so it is known today.

A grateful government rewarded Edward Jenner with grants totaling thirty-thousand pounds. France and England erected monuments to him. From America came a grateful letter from Indian tribes long ravaged by smallpox.

Dr. Edward Jenner lived to see the fruits of his labors applied throughout the world, although long years of debate remained in some areas to hinder the advance of vaccination. He died peacefully at home on January 25, 1823, at the age of seventy-three.

8

Merciful Sleep

Pain was the great barrier.

Hippocrates, Galen, Paré, and hundreds of lesser doctors had known it was possible to help the human body through injury and illness by surgical means. But unendurable pain made it impossible to accomplish very much.

Tumors were cut out and hemorrhoids were removed in the time of Hippocrates; Galen sewed together the cut tendons and wounds of his gladiators; Paré amputated the limbs of his wounded soldiers—and men and women screamed in agony as the knife touched them, for there was no such thing as anesthetic to take away the pain.

The patient was strapped to the operating table

or held down by strong assistants. An operation could not be allowed to last more than two or three minutes. If it lasted as long as fifteen minutes the patient died of pain and shock.

Until little more than a hundred years ago there was almost no relief for pain of any kind, whether caused by injury, surgery, or childbirth. Certain drugs and herbs were tried with little success. Alcohol was often used. The ordeal of an operation was almost as terrible for a sensitive doctor as it was for the patient. Sometimes the surgeon went into the operating room with two bottles of whiskey in his pockets, one for the patient and one for himself.

Charles Darwin, the great naturalist, once had dreams of becoming a doctor—until he witnessed a surgical operation. The horror of it quickly changed his mind.

Doctors since the days of Hippocrates had dreamed of ways to kill pain. The dream seemed hopeless.

The man who finally made that dream come true was an American dentist, William T. G. Morton.

On the morning of Friday, October 16, 1846, William Morton was due at the Massachusetts General Hospital in Boston. Dr. John Collins Warren, the most eminent surgeon in New England, had offered him the privilege of demonstrating at a surgical operation an invention which he claimed would lessen the sensation of pain.

The great surgeon was sixty-eight years old at the time. William Morton was twenty-seven. The invention was ether anesthesia and a means of administering it to a patient.

William had been notified of the date of the operation only two days previously and was working until early morning to improve an inhalation apparatus which he had invented. His young wife, Elizabeth, was helping, but she was in a state of exhaustion from her great anxiety.

William looked up from his work as she leaned against the table a moment and closed her eyes. "Please go to bed," he said. "I'll be finished soon. You're making yourself sick."

"No," said Elizabeth unsteadily. "You are the one who should sleep. You are due at the hospital in only a few hours. Forget this inhaler. The one Mr. Chamberlain is making for you will do."

He patted her shoulder. "There's just one more thing I want to try. The demonstration tomorrow must be perfect. I simply can't risk any chance of failing."

Elizabeth hesitated to speak of her fears, but she could not hold them back. "Then perhaps you should not take the risk at all. Oh, William, I couldn't endure it if anything happened to you!"

"Why, what could possibly happen to me?" William put his arms about his wife and held her closely. "Nothing can happen."

"You know perfectly well what could happen. If you fail, you'll be ridiculed to death. But that would be the least disaster. If the patient should die you would be arrested for manslaughter and sent to prison. That's the risk you take!"

William Morton was very still as he continued to hold his wife close. "Then that is the risk I must take," he said. "I have proved that ether is safe and effective in extraction of teeth. I know I am right in believing it will be every bit as effective in surgical operations. I've got to prove it. I've got to show them!"

In spite of her fears, Elizabeth had confidence in her young husband. She wanted him to succeed. If only the risk were not so great. . . .

At two o'clock in the morning William gave up his attempts on the improved inhaler. The one Chamberlain was making would have to do, but he felt sure it would not be finished if he didn't get down there and prod the cranky old instrument maker.

He arose at dawn after a few hours' rest, and said good-bye to Elizabeth. She watched from the window as he strode toward the instrument shop. She did not know what this day would bring for her husband—acclaim as a genius or arrest as a criminal.

William was right about Chamberlain. There was several hours' work yet to do on the inhaler. This was a simple device consisting of a spherical container with an open mouth on one side near the top, and a tube on the other side. A valve in the tube permitted the vapor of ether mixed with air to be drawn out as a patient inhaled, but prevented the breath from being exhaled into the container.

The airtight fastening of the tube to the glass chamber seemed beyond Chamberlain's powers that morning. He worked at it reluctantly under William's anxious urging.

Shortly before ten o'clock another man entered the shop. It was Eben Frost, a music teacher for whom William had extracted a tooth with the use of ether only a few days before. He was to go along to the hospital as a witness to the safety of ether.

"It's almost ten," said Eben anxiously. "The operation will start in a few minutes."

William was sick at heart. "I know," he said. He pleaded with Chamberlain. "Please hurry. I should be at the hospital now."

Chamberlain looked up with antagonism. "You can finish it yourself if you want to."

William groaned and sat down while he watched the unhurried hands of the instrument maker. The clock on the wall showed ten.

"I guess you can take it now," said Chamberlain a moment later.

Without a word, William grabbed the inhaler and raced out the door. Eben Frost followed.

The hospital was blocks away, but they ran the whole distance and took the stone steps leading to the entrance two at a time. In the corridor William slowed to catch his breath. His heart was pounding frantically. He and Eben entered the operating amphitheatre just as Dr. Warren raised his scalpel.

The operating amphitheater was crowded with students and other doctors, as was usual when Dr. Warren was operating. A few minutes before ten the patient had been brought in. He was Gilbert Abbot, a twenty-year-old printer, who had a tumor below his left jaw. He had volunteered on the previous Tuesday to permit the use of William Morton's new discovery in the removal of the tumor.

He was led into the room wearing light trousers and a shirt open at the neck. A surgical chair was to be used. He was strapped into it.

Dr. Warren turned to the audience. "This morning, gentlemen, we are to use a new method, recently perfected by Dr. William Morton, a dentist of this city, for permitting an operation to be performed while keeping the patient free from pain."

An astonished murmur rippled through the audience. They had not expected to witness any such experiment as this!

Dr. Warren looked at the clock impatiently and at the door through which William Morton had not appeared. He began to show signs of irritation. Finally, at a quarter after ten he gave up. He said sarcastically, "As Dr. Morton has not arrived, I presume he is otherwise engaged."

The audience laughed. They knew the kind of quacks that pretended to such discoveries. Dr. Warren approached the nervous patient. It had been too good to be true, thought Gilbert Abbott. He steeled himself and closed his eyes to receive the burning pain of the surgeon's knife-thrust. The onlookers tensed for the expected screams.

At that moment William Morton and Eben Frost entered the amphitheater. Dr. Warren looked up angrily. William tried to apologize and explain his lateness.

The surgeon backed away coldly, brushing away

the explanations. He extended a hand toward Gilbert and said to Morton. "Well, sir, your patient is ready."

All trace of anxiety and haste was gone from William Morton now. He approached the young printer with a smile and began filling the inhaler from a bottle of ether he had carried in his pocket. "This man is Eben Frost," he said to Gilbert. "I brought him along because he has already inhaled ether without suffering harm, and I pulled a tooth while he was asleep."

"It didn't hurt a bit," said Eben. "You won't feel a thing."

"I hope not," said Gilbert.

"Are you afraid?" William asked.

Gilbert shook his head. "No."

William put the inhaler to Gilbert's mouth. "Breathe deeply through the tube. That is all."

After a few minutes, Gilbert Abbott's head sagged. William held the tube close to his nostrils so that he might continue breathing the fumes. At last, he stepped back and spoke to the surgeon. "*Your* patient is ready, Doctor."

There was utter stillness in the room. Dr. Warren took up the knife once more. The operation was not dangerous, but it was ordinarily extremely painful. The audience could not believe there would not be a shrill cry as soon as the knife made its incision and the operation began.

There was no cry. A three-inch incision was opened. The nerves and blood vessels were laid aside. The tumor was exposed and quickly removed. Gilbert Abbott remained still as if sleeping peacefully most of the time. Only toward the last did he stir restlessly.

The wound was closed and the blood washed away. The operation had taken about half an hour.

When Gilbert was conscious again, William Morton was the first to speak to him. "Did you feel any pain?"

Gilbert's voice was thick from the anesthetic. "Feels like m'neck's been scratched," he said.

"You felt nothing during the operation?" Warren asked.

"I was aware of the operation, but I didn't feel pain at all."

Dr. Warren expelled a deep breath and turned to the motionless audience. "Gentlemen," he said, "this is no humbug!"

Was there ever a greater moment in all of man's experience in healing?

Hippocrates, Galen, Vesalius, Harvey—all of them had made tremendous contributions to the knowledge and understanding of the human body. But, until the shrieks of agony from the operating room could be banished forever, that knowledge had limited use. With one great stride, William Morton had fought back the dark curtains of pain that kept previous surgeons from ministering to their fellow men.

But the story of William Morton's remaining lifetime is a strange and tragic one. On the day of his great triumph he felt no elation. Elizabeth Morton later described that day in which she sat by the window of their home for twelve "hours of mortal anxiety," and her shock at William's appearance as he returned.

"His usually genial face was so sad," she wrote,

"that I felt failure must have come. He took me in his arms, almost fainting as I was, and said tenderly, 'Well, dear, I succeeded.'

"In spite of these words his gloom . . . made it impossible for me to believe the good news. He should have been highly elated at having accomplished one of the most splendid achievements of the century, and yet, there he was, sick at heart. . . . This was not due to bodily fatigue but to an intuitive perception of the troubles in store for him. It is literally true that Dr. Morton was never the same man after that day; his whole life was embittered through the priceless boon he had conferred upon the human race."

These words of Elizabeth Morton are a faithful description of what befell her husband. Why it should have been so is a question that has fascinated and puzzled historians for three-quarters of a century.

Dr. William Morton gave the principle of anesthesia to the world, but there were other men on the fringes of the great discovery.

Ether was first prepared in the thirteenth century by a Spanish alchemist, Raymond Lull. Two hundred years later, Paracelsus, a doctor and alchemist, observed that chickens could be put to sleep by it.

The great English scientist Humphrey Davy, who discovered nitrous oxide which came to be called "laughing gas," wrote in 1800, "As nitrous oxide . . . seems capable of destroying physical pain, it may probably be used with advantage during surgical operations."

He never tried it.

Faraday, Davy's student and successor, wrote in 1818, "When the vapour of ether is . . . inhaled, it produces effects very similar to those occasioned by nitrous oxide. By the incautious breathing of ether vapour, a man was thrown into a lethargic condition which . . . lasted for thirty hours."

Faraday did nothing about it, either.

A few years after Faraday's observation, students in both England and America discovered that ether had an intoxicating effect, and "ether parties" became a fad. In Georgia, in 1842, Crawford W. Long, a young country doctor, observed the effect produced by ether at these parties, and he wondered about a possible medical use for the effect. He persuaded a friend to let him remove a tumor on the neck while the friend was insensible from ether. Dr. Long could hardly believe the wonderful results of this experiment.

He performed a total of eight minor operations with the use of ether anesthetic. But he had enemies, and the people of the neighborhood were superstitious. They called on him and told him to give up this unnatural practice and warned that if he should accidentally kill someone with the ether he would be lynched.

Dr. Long bowed to the superstitions of his neighbors and abandoned his experiments. His discovery lay buried in the backwoods of Georgia.

During these years, traveling lecturers gave exhibitions of the effects of "laughing gas" and invited members of their audiences to inhale. In 1844 a young dentist, Horace Wells, of Hartford, Connecticut, witnessed one of the demonstrations. He noticed that those who inhaled seemed to be unaware of the bruises and bumps resulting from their intoxicated actions. Wells immediately saw the possible use of nitrous oxide as an aid to dentistry. A few days later he submitted to inhalation of the gas, and a fellow dentist pulled one of his teeth. Wells could scarcely believe the absence of pain.

"A new era in tooth-pulling!" he cried.

He made a number of "painless" extractions in others, then set out for Boston to give a demonstration to Harvard professors and students. The demonstration failed because he gave too little gas, and he was ridiculed unmercifully. Wells abandoned dentistry altogether and turned to business ventures, which were unsuccessful, one after another.

William Thomas Green Morton was born in 1819 in the New England farm community of Charleton, Massachusetts, not far west of Boston. He was driven by a thirst for knowledge and learning, but the early failure of his father's country store prevented his achieving his desire to go to medical school. He chose dentistry, instead. At that time, dentistry required a minimum of specialized education, as surgery did in the time of Ambroise Paré.

William Morton went into partnership with Horace Wells in Boston in 1843; the partnership lasted about a year. Wells returned to Hartford, but he and Morton remained friends. Later, he asked William's help in arranging the ill-fated Harvard demonstration of nitrous oxide.

During their partnership the dentists became acquainted with a strange character, Dr. Charles Thomas Jackson. Out of the depths of a great mental illness Jackson was to become an incredible enemy of William Morton and literally drive him to his grave. But when the young dentists first met him, Jackson was a well-educated, respected scientist, who sometimes lectured on medical subjects at Harvard.

William took some medical courses at Harvard at this time and studied under Jackson. He and his young wife Elizabeth even lived at the Jackson home for a time.

William, like many dentists of his time, was searching for a means of painless extraction of teeth. He questioned Jackson, who had a good knowledge of chemistry, and Jackson suggested the application of a few drops of ether to the tooth and surrounding tissue.

William tried this on a patient and found it useful. Then, after witnessing the failure of his former partner Horace Wells, he wondered about the possibility of inhalation of ether vapor. He studied the existing textbooks, obtained what information was available from people who had witnessed ether parties, and he discussed the qualities of ether with Dr. Jackson.

Jackson suggested pure sulphuric ether as the only reliable type for such experiments, but he warned William not to try such things in his dental practice lest he get involved in the kind of "humbug" that Wells had ended with.

William ignored the warning and continued his experiments on himself and on his wife's pet dog and other animals. Then, on September 30, 1846, the music teacher Eben Frost appeared at his door late one evening with a terrible toothache and a plea for something to relieve him. He asked if he could be hypnotized and have the tooth pulled. William told him he had something much better.

After a few breaths of ether, Eben Frost became unconscious. When he recovered, he was astonished to see his extracted tooth on the floor.

William Morton knew then that he had the long-sought discovery in his hands. He applied to no less than the great leading surgeon of Massachusetts General Hospital, the renowned Dr. Warren, for an opportunity to prove his discovery. Doctors of that day were wearied with crackpot ideas regarding painless operations, but Dr. Warren was open-minded enough to give William his chance.

On that day in 1846 a new era in medicine opened.

Almost immediately, Dr. C. T. Jackson set about to play his incredible part in the drama. Jackson was a man of education but of little achievement. He had failed to attract patients as a physician and had turned to chemistry and geology. He envied the achievements of others. His mental illness was demonstrated by his efforts to claim their work for his own.

Samuel F. B. Morse, who invented the telegraph and the Morse code, had earlier fought off Jackson's attacks for seven years, for Jackson had claimed that he, not Morse, was the inventor. At another time Jackson claimed that the invention of gun-cotton was his and not that of its inventor, C. F. Schonbein. He had tried to steal a share of the accomplishments of a great physiologist of his time, William Beaumont. He even made some claims to discoveries that related to the circulation of the blood.

Defeated in all these attempts, he now saw in the work of William Morton a chance for glory, fame, and riches. He leaped to the attack.

He claimed the discovery of ether anesthesia for himself. He claimed that he had disclosed information about it to his surgeon friends in Boston long ago, and that he had sent William Morton to Dr. Warren to have it tested. Dr. Warren testified that he had never heard of it before William Morton revealed it.

Jackson stirred up claims for Horace Wells; he unearthed the forgotten work of Crawford Long in Georgia. When Morton presented his claims to the Academy of Sciences in Paris for recognition and approval, Jackson was already there with his own claims.

Congress had made substantial grants to Samuel Morse for his invention of the telegraph. William Morton appealed for grants to partly reimburse him for the funds and time that had gone into his work. President Pierce promised that the grant would be given.

Jackson's maneuvering blocked it.

The torment broke William's health, but the persistence that had led him to the revelation of anesthesia to the world now led him to fight back. It would have been better if he had not, for Jackson would eventually have worn himself out. As it was, he wore William out.

Jackson destroyed William's remaining dental practice by sending false claims and lawsuits to William's patients for bills already paid. William lost his home through lawsuits and creditors' claims sponsored by Jackson. He was reduced on one occasion to bargaining with a baker for bread for his family in exchange for a cartful of wood.

This incredible attack by Jackson went on for

twenty years. The final blow was struck in 1868. William and Elizabeth were in Washington, still making futile attempts to obtain government recognition and grants, when a new magazine article by Jackson appeared. William was deathly ill at the time, and the article inflamed his old anger beyond control. He left immediately for New York to prepare a counterattack, against the protests of Elizabeth and his doctors.

A few days later he wired Elizabeth to come at once; he was ill. After he was on his feet once more, but still sick, he asked Elizabeth to go for an evening carriage drive to escape the terrible July heat.

They drove through Central Park, and William stopped the carriage. He jumped out and stood a moment as if in great pain, then collapsed on the ground. After hours had elapsed, the police and others finally helped Elizabeth get him to the hospital.

There, the chief surgeon recognized William Morton immediately. "This is Dr. Morton?" he asked Elizabeth.

She nodded. "Yes."

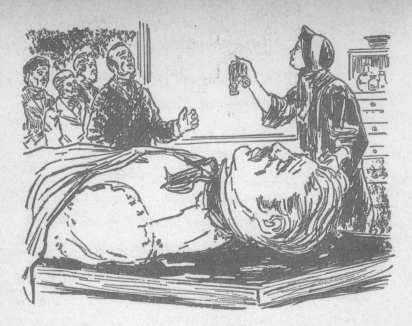

The doctor turned to the resident pupils, who had gathered about. "Young gentlemen," he said, "you see lying before you a man who has done more for humanity and for the relief of suffering than any man who has ever lived."

Bitterly, with tears in her eyes, Elizabeth took out of her pocket three medals which had been given William by Russia, Norway and Sweden, and France. "Yes," she said, "and here is all the recompense he ever received for it."

He received a little more. He was buried with a noble monument over his grave, which reads:

William Thomas Green Morton
Inventor. Revealer of Anaesthetic Inhalation.
By whom pain in surgery was averted
and annulled.
Before whom in all time surgery was agony.
Since whom science has control of pain.

Crawford Long lived out his years full of bitter regret that he had hidden his discovery from the world. He was a broken old man when, in 1878, a farmer knocked on the door of his house. "Doctor —my wife—she's in labor. You've got to help. She can't stand the pain. . . ."

Dr. Crawford Long could not resist. He put a small bottle of ether in his pocket and went to the farmer's house. As he was about to administer the anesthetic to the agonized woman, he collapsed and died.

Horace Wells had sunk further into despair after the business failures which followed his abandonment of dentistry. He formed the habit of easing his mental anguish with chloroform intoxication.

One night in January, 1848, under the influence of it, he was arrested and thrown into prison. There, he further inhaled to the point of insensibility, but he held a razor ready until he felt himself on the thin edge of unconsciousness. Then he slashed a great artery in his leg and bled to death.

One summer day in 1873, Dr. C. T. Jackson wandered through the Boston cemetery and came upon the monument to William Morton. He had destroyed the man, but he could not destroy the memory or the record in stone, which was there for all the world to see. His illness of mind swelled up in total madness and he struck at the monument with his bare hands, clawing and shrieking the name of the man he hated above all else in the world.

Jackson was taken away and lodged in the McLean Asylum for the insane, where he died in 1880 at the age of seventy-five.

Relief from pain had come into the world, but the process had brought tragedy into the lives of every man who had even the smallest part in it.

9

The Little Killers

There seems to be no limit to the strange notions the mind of man can contain. In ancient Egypt, when frogs emerged from the muddy flats of the overflowing Nile, men supposed the frogs grew out of the mud itself, without parent frogs to give them birth. Only a few hundred years ago, a respected scientist performed an experiment which showed —he said—that mice could be produced by placing scraps of linen and some cheese in a box and leaving it alone for a while! It didn't occur to him that the mice were attracted from other parts of the house and climbed into the box to get the cheese.

One of the biggest arguments in favor of spontaneous generation of life, as this process was called, was the fact that meat left in the open air in warm weather would soon be crawling with little white worms called maggots. Where did the maggots come from? From the decaying meat, of course, was the belief.

An Italian experimenter named Francesco Redi covered the meat so that flies could not get to it to lay their eggs. When this was done the meat remained free of maggots, which are simply the larvae of flies. For a long time, this simple experiment served to kill the doctrine of spontaneous generation. Then Leeuwenhoek discovered his millions of "little animals" and the theory sprang up all over again. Where did the little animals come from? They just grew out of whatever substance they were found to be on, that's all. *They* didn't need any parents! So the argument went on.

Serious scientists as late as 1910 taught that microscopic life could originate by spontaneous generation. In the 1860's and 1870's the question of spontaneous generation was debated furiously, and an agreement on the matter was extremely important to the proper understanding of microscopic life and its relationship to man.

In 1859 a young French chemist named Louis Pasteur told himself and his friends, "It's time for this question to be settled once and for all. It's preposterous that sober men of science should believe such nonsense as spontaneous generation!"

His scientist friends, older men who had taught him as a youth, warned him to stay out of the conflict.

"It's useless," they said. "The theory may be false, but you'll only waste your time trying to prove it, and you'll make enemies as well. Work at something useful; let spontaneous generation alone!"

But Louis Pasteur, at thirty-seven, was already a veteran of fierce scientific battles. He had proven, in the face of opposition from the entire scientific world, that microorganisms, Leeuwenhoek's "little animals," were responsible for the chemical changes which occur in fermentation—the process that produces alcohols, wines, and acids from vegetable matter—and in putrefaction, which is seen in decaying meat, the rotting of vegetation, and the production of pus in a wound of the body. His developing theories of microscopic life demanded an end to the ridiculous notion of spontaneous generation.

Professor F. A. Pouchet had written, "By meditation, it became evident to me that spontaneous generation was one of the means employed by nature for the reproduction of living things. I applied myself to discover the methods by which this takes place."

He reported to the Paris Academy of Sciences that he was able to demonstrate at will that microscopic life could be generated in bottles completely sealed against germs that might enter from outside. He had also proven, he said, that the air contains no living organisms at all.

To Louis Pasteur, this was a declaration of war. With the microscope, Louis had *seen* germs taken from the air of his own laboratory. He would prove that germs would not grow in a solution in a bottle until they were introduced from outside.

But how?

A renowned chemist friend, Antoine Balard, was visiting in Louis's laboratory and listening as the younger man paced up and down repeating his angry question and accusing Pouchet of all kinds of stupidity.

"Suppose you try this," said Balard quietly. "Prepare a flask of nutrient yeast fluid, which has a tube in the neck of it shaped like an S, or like the neck of a swan. Up and down, then up again. Like so." His hand made a graceful swoop through the air.

Louis halted his frantic pacing. His eyes lighted. "I see it! Sterilize the yeast solution and the flask by heating. Then the air of the room will be sucked back into the flask as the flask cools."

"And I think," said Balard, "that you will find the fluid will remain sterile. No fermentation will appear in the yeast, even though it is not only unsealed, but is quite open to the air of the room."

"I'm sure you are right!" said Louis. "The air will enter, but dust and germs will fall to the bottom of the curved tube and will not rise to be carried up into the yeast solution. That will prove that fermentation can be caused only by something in the air, and that this something can be kept out of the fluid by so simple a means as the curved tube!"

The experiment showed results exactly as Balard

and Louis Pasteur predicted. The yeast remained sterile until the S tube was removed. Then fermentation and germ growth quickly appeared. This proved to them that germ-laden dust, settling out of the air, was the cause of new germ life starting to grow in the fluid.

The demonstration failed to satisfy Pouchet and his colleagues. "There couldn't possibly be enough germs in the air to account for the heavy bacterial growth obtainable in the laboratory," said Pouchet. "If so, the air would be as dense as iron with the germ life it carried. Your experiment actually proves spontaneous generation, for it is the oxygen of the air that makes it possible."

How to silence this foolish gibbering?

Well, there would be a way. Louis prepared twenty-one sterile flasks of yeast solution and sealed the tops by drawing the tips out and sealing them with an alcohol lamp.

He grinned at his assistant, Duclaux. "You wonder how this will confound Pouchet? Help me with these boxes of flasks out to the carriage and I will show you."

They took ten flasks to the basement of the Paris Observatory and opened them in the cool, calm air. Then they quickly sealed the tips again. Outside, near the dusty street, they did the same with the remaining eleven. Then they hurried back to the laboratory.

After the elapse of sufficient time for germs to incubate in the flasks, Louis exclaimed in triumph. "Exactly as I thought! Only one flask opened in the basement shows any signs of germ life. But all eleven flasks opened near the dusty street are contaminated!

"That proves it," he continued to Duclaux. "Don't you see? If oxygen in the air caused germs to appear spontaneously, there would be equal growth in all flasks. But if germs in the air are the cause, then it is to be expected that the air in some places will have more germs than the air in others. And so it is!"

Even the common people of France became excited by this great scientific controversy. A magazine editor wrote, "What will be the outcome of this giants' struggle?"

One outcome was that Louis found himself clinging to a narrow trail on the side of a mountain in
the Swiss Alps, trying to keep a stubborn donkey
from falling over the edge of a precipice and carrying
with it a load of precious sealed flasks. Freezing
winds howled across the crags, and Louis was blue
with cold.

He was determined, however, to show without
question how great were the differences in germ
content of the air. At the top of this ice-coated
mountain he expected to show that the air was
almost completely free of germs.

The Swiss guide had seen many crazy French-
men, but none quite like this. "*Monsieur,* you wish
me to take you to the top of the mountain with
thirty-two bottles? And you are merely to open and
close them again? *Monsieur,* if you wish to go mountain climbing I will take you to the very top of the
Montanvert, but as for the bottles, let us be sensible
men and open them right here! No?"

"No," said Louis. "On the mountain. Must I get
another guide?"

"Of course not." The guide smiled broadly now.

"But the money in advance, if you please. My wife, you know— She takes care of it. Just in case anything should happen on the mountain. . . ."

Louis saw nothing dramatic or extraordinary about the trip, but he was exasperated as he tried to reseal his flasks in the icy wind. The lamp was worse than useless, but he refused to shield the flame for fear of dropping germs into the flask from the shielding material.

"I must return to the village and modify the lamp," said Louis. "We will try again tomorrow. By then, perhaps the wind will be less."

The guide shook his head gloomily. The crazy Frenchman would never stand another trip up this mountain. But then, if he was willing to pay in advance. . . .

"The wind is never less on the mountain," he said.

In spite of the hardships of this trip, Louis managed to open and reseal twenty of his flasks. Back in the warmth of the village inn, he watched the results. Perfect! Only one of the twenty showed any sign of germ growth in the liquid. The other nineteen remained completely sterile. That should settle Pouchet's silly argument about the oxygen of the air being responsible for generation of germs.

It didn't. However, Louis did not hear of Pouchet again for a long time—almost three years. Then he read a report that Pouchet and his friends had climbed to the foot of a Swiss glacier, the Maladetta, much higher than Louis had gone. Louis remembered his own hardships and sympathized with his rivals. One of them had been almost killed on the return trip.

But Pouchet reported that every one of his flasks he had taken had been invaded by germ life on the glacier!

"This must stop!" exclaimed Louis. "These men do not even know how to conduct a precise scientific experiment!"

Pouchet seemed sincere enough. He suggested that both groups put on a public demonstration before the Academy of Sciences. Louis accepted with delight. Then Pouchet's group asked for a postponement. Then another. Finally, they withdrew altogether.

Louis did not wish to call off the demonstration, however. He demanded that it proceed, and the Academy agreed. They appointed a commission, and Louis prepared sixty flasks.

Louis had three unused flasks from his mountain journey of three years before. They were still as sterile as the day he sealed them. In the laboratory of the Museum of Natural History the scientist opened one of these before the commission. Within three days, this flask showed abundant growth of germ life.

Louis opened nineteen of his flasks in the lecture hall of the museum. Five of these developed germ growth. He led the commission to the dome of the building and opened nineteen more. Six developed growth. Outside, near the dusty boulevard, he opened eighteen. Of these, sixteen became contaminated.

Louis had proved his point as far as the Academy was concerned. They said there was no evidence in support of spontaneous generation of life. Rather, all experimental evidence pointed to the fact that growth of microorganisms appeared only after the introduction of a microorganism from some other source.

But Louis was not concerned with the matter of spontaneous generation alone. He was thinking at this time far beyond that question. He wrote later, "What would be most desirable would be to push those studies far enough to prepare the road for a serious research into the origin of the various diseases."

The events of his life seemed to lead him naturally in this direction. In 1865 he was asked to undertake one of the strangest endeavors ever presented to a scientist. He was requested to cure some sick worms!

These were very important worms, however—silkworms. For many decades, silk production had been a major industry in France and now was worth five million dollars a year to the French farmers. But the worms were sick. Some kind of disease that produced strange, pepperlike spots was destroying them.

"But I know nothing about silkworms!" Louis protested to his friend, the chemist Dumas, who had brought word of the government's request. "I have never even seen a silkworm!"

"You will," said Dumas. "You will."

Louis read a book about silkworms while traveling on the train to Alais, the region where he was to study the disease for the next four summers.

He undertook the task for two reasons: the economic importance of the silk industry to his beloved France, and the scientific challenge of the problem itself. He saw in the illness of the silkworms another evidence of the action of the "little animals" that hover everywhere, ready to strike man or animal with disease.

Louis had to contend with the disbelief of the farmers of Alais. "We ask the government for help," they cried, "and we receive one poor schoolteacher, who has never seen a silkworm in his whole life! What kind of help is that?"

But slowly Louis won them over. He proposed programs of examination of healthy worms and isolation from diseased ones. The farmers reluctantly agreed to cooperate. There was little else they could do under the circumstances.

But failure followed every effort. Season after season, the silkworm crop diminished, until there was little left. Then Louis discovered he had the same kind of problem that had perplexed Edward Jenner in his cowpox experiments eighty years before. The silkworms did not have just one disease; they had two!

With this discovery, Louis succeeded in devising a plan through which the farmers could safely segregate the sick worms from the healthy ones. After four years of painstaking work, he saved the French silk industry.

At the same time he was working on the silkworm problem, he was asked to help the wine industry of France. The wines were sick, too. They spoiled and turned to vinegar.

With his experience in the problems of pollution by germs in the air, Louis had little difficulty in showing that the spoilage was caused by microorganisms from the air. But how to get rid of them?

The answer suddenly, one day, seemed very simple. "Heat," he said to his laboratory assistant. "Heat will kill the germs. All we have to do is to heat the wines and seal them up. This will stop the spoilage."

"But the heat will spoil the wine, too," his assistant protested. "And how hot must it be to kill the germs? How long must it be heated?"

"That's what experiments are for," said Louis. "We will experiment until we find the answers to those questions."

They found the right answers. Today the same process is applied to milk and other products to kill germs. We would not think of drinking milk that had not been treated this way. We call the process pasteurization.

A great darkness fell upon Louis Pasteur and all of France in the years that followed. In 1870, the Prussian Bismarck led his troops across French soil and ravaged and destroyed the towns and countryside. Louis was too old—forty-eight—and he was handicapped by a partial paralysis of one side of his body. The French army could not accept him.

He continued his work on fermentation as best he could during these bitter years. Then, in 1873, Louis was elected to the Academy of Medicine. The election gave him an opportunity he had longed for, an opportunity to influence men of medicine with the new ideas that were in his mind.

In speeches before the Academy, this brand-new member, who was not a doctor at all, urged the doctors to begin a search for the germs of disease. "These are the little killers that cause sickness!" he said. "Find ways to destroy them and you will save thousands of lives."

Louis had been elected to the Academy by a majority of only one vote. The doctors were not anxious to hear him. "That chemist!" they said. "Who is he that he should be telling us how to practice medicine?"

Alone, except for young laboratory assistants who worked long and loyally with him, Louis pursued his search for the connection between microbes—a term that had recently been invented by one of his friends—and disease. He filled his laboratory with animals and fowls and began experiments on cholera in chickens.

Edward Jenner's method of vaccination for smallpox had been in use for several decades, but no one really understood why it worked, nor had similar methods been found for other diseases. With this in mind, Louis turned to his cholera experiments.

Completely by accident, he discovered an astounding fact. The germ which he used to infect chickens with experimental doses of cholera were normally expected to kill them. But one day he found a batch of chickens quite healthy and alive when they should have been dead of the disease.

He pondered, then observed. "The germ culture used to infect these chickens was an old one," he said to his assistants. "It was too weak to give the disease fatally. Let us use the strongest batch of cholera germs we have and see what happens."

What happened was that the chickens were entirely immune to any cholera germs that Louis and his assistants could pour into them. Louis quickly realized that in this simple manner he had found the thing he had so long sought. By weakening the germs and infecting chickens with them, he could make the chickens only mildly ill—and render them immune thereafter to the most powerful germs of the disease. He called the process vaccination, as the process of immunization from smallpox was called.

At the Academy of Medicine he enthusiastically reported his findings. But instead of sharing his enthusiasm, most of the dignified physicians were either bored or angered by his discussion of chickens.

"But don't you see?" cried Louis as they scorned him. "What we have found to be true of chicken cholera can also be applied to human disease. Thousands of children will be saved from typhoid, diphtheria, and other diseases when we find the right vaccines. Won't you ever open your blind, unseeing eyes?"

"Take your silly chickens away to the farm!" they told him.

Louis left the Academy of Medicine, but derision had never made him retreat and it didn't do so now. He plunged back into laboratory work, this time to attack one of the deadliest diseases of his time, anthrax. This disease killed millions of dollars' worth of cattle and sheep in all parts of the world every year. It could attack human beings, too, with agonizing and fatal results.

Sleepless for long periods, Louis Pasteur and his assistants worked at the problem. It was far more difficult than the cholera problem. The anthrax germs would not weaken but remained capable of killing, no matter how old they were. It was known that sheep could become fatally diseased simply by grazing on land where the disease had been present years before.

Yet, at last, a method was found. Mild heat would do the trick. They tried the weakened solution on sheep. By experimenting they found the right dosage that would not harm sheep but would protect them against the deadly disease. Louis took his announcement this time to the Academy of Science.

One of Louis's strongest opponents was M. Rossignol, a veterinarian. With cunning and disbelief in Louis's methods, he laid a trap. He wrote to the *Veterinary Press,* a magazine which he helped edit, and urged a public demonstration. "This," he said, "will strike every mind and convince those who may still be doubting; the evidence of facts will have the result of ending all uncertainty."

He expected a public failure, which would crush Louis Pasteur forever.

Louis scented battle, and with some recklessness agreed to the terms of the demonstration. Cows were to be included, although the vaccine had never been tested on cattle.

The summer of 1881 saw the test take place at a farm called Pouilly le Fort. The vaccination of James Phipps by Edward Jenner was scarcely more dramatic and tense than was the vaccination of the sheep and cows at Pouilly le Fort that summer. The entire reputation and career of Louis Pasteur rested on the outcome.

At last, when the time came for the final test to determine if the animals would survive a dose of the deadliest anthrax germs, it seemed as if all the leading scientists of France were present.

Louis Pasteur got out of the carriage that had brought him from the railroad station to the farm. He made his way slowly through the crowd that parted before him. Everything was silent. No one spoke. In his heart he dreaded seeing the results. Were the vaccinated animals dead?

Then his final steps took him through the edge of the crowd and he saw the animals.

The unvaccinated test animals—twenty-four sheep—were dead, except for two that were almost dead.

But every one of the vaccinated animals was alive and healthy—both sheep and cows.

Suddenly a long cheer and a burst of applause went up from the crowd. Louis felt a surge of relief and gratitude that almost choked him. This was the greatest triumph of his entire career. It was one of the great triumphs of human history.

The method of vaccination spread quickly to other diseases. Louis soon perfected a vaccine for rabies, one of the deadly scourges of his day, which was widely spread by wild dogs and wolves.

Singlehanded, with the support of a handful of loyal friends, Louis Pasteur had broken the barrier that prevented man's understanding and conquest of disease and infection throughout the centuries. Alone, he had proposed and proved that the "little animals," the germs, the microbes, were responsible for infectious disease, each disease produced by one particular germ. He proved, then, that these germs could be conquered by vaccines.

He had been a fierce and vigorous fighter all his life. If he had not been, he would have succumbed to the attacks thrust at him. But he lived to see the honors of the world poured upon him before he died at the age of seventy-three in September, 1895.

10

The Old Black Frock Coat

In 1850 the surgery of the University College
Hospital in London was a small room equipped with
an ancient wooden operating table, a cabinet of instruments, a small wash basin, and a single gas jet
for light.

Two young students watched the surgeon prepare to operate. He hung his street coat on a hanger
and put on his operating coat. This was an old black
frock coat that had been removed long ago from
his wardrobe at home because it was worn out.
When he was a very young surgeon he had set it
aside as his operating coat.

He had used it now for twenty years, the same
coat. It was blood-stained and spotted with pus

discharged from wounds of patients of years ago. These spots he wore proudly as badges of honor to his long practice of surgery.

One of the medical students nudged the other and nodded toward the ancient coat. "Some day," he said, "I'm going to have one just like that. Don't you wish you owned such a coat, Joseph?"

Joseph Lister shook his head. "If I did, I'd burn it!"

His companion glared indignantly. "There's not a medical student in all England who wouldn't give his right arm, almost, for the privilege of owning and wearing a coat like that. You don't get one of those without years of practice in surgery!"

Joseph Lister watched the surgeon check the supply of sutures threaded in the lapel of the coat. They, too, were stained. Dried blood from perhaps several previous operations marked them.

"It ought to be burned," Joseph Lister repeated.

"You're crazy!"

"Perhaps. But the least to be expected of a surgeon is that he does not shed crusts of dried blood and pus in his patient's wounds as he operates!"

Surgeons of a hundred years ago cannot be great-ly blamed for their attitudes. An operation was a horribly messy thing at best. True, in the years since Ambroise Paré, surgeons had learned much and had gained considerable skill. The discovery of anesthet-ics had enabled them to perform operations that would have seemed little short of miraculous only a few years before.

But in an operation blood flowed and spattered clothes and instruments, and within hours the wound was full of yellow, foul-smelling pus. An operating room was simply a place where very dirty work was performed. Why try to keep the place clean? It was as ridiculous as suggesting today that an auto mechanic dress in clean, white clothes for each automobile repair and keep his garage spot-less.

The old, black frock coat was a very practical garment for such messy work as operating. So the surgeons of yesterday thought.

But in spite of anesthesia and the most advanced skills, surgeons could scarcely count their profession a successful one. Death seemed to guide their hands.

At least forty-five percent of amputations were still fatal. Head and chest operations were not to be thought of. Surgeons looked with horror on the mere idea of opening the abdomen. Only a few of the most desperate ever tried it, generally with fatal results.

Pus formation, like bleeding, was considered a normal part of the problem. Almost every wound which broke the skin, either by accident or the surgeon's knife, reeked with pus within a few hours. Most physicians and surgeons considered it a part of the healing process. At the time of Hippocrates it was known as "laudable pus." But Hippocrates was not convinced that it was necessary. He had observed a few rare cases where pus did not form and the wound healed cleanly with only a thin line to mark the place where it had been. He called this "healing by first intention."

In 1854, Joseph Lister visited such a case with his student friend, Batty Tuke. Joseph said, "The main object in my life is to find out how to procure such a result in all wounds."

This was a tremendous goal, for when Joseph

Lister was a student, healing by first intention was almost unknown.

After the formation of pus, most wounds were afflicted with one of several "hospital diseases," as they were called. Erysipelas was one of these. It caused large patches of skin to become hot with fever, red, and thick. Inflammation of the heart or lungs or brain often followed. It was extremely dangerous and usually fatal.

Pyemia was a disease in which infected blood clots traveled to distant parts of the body and set up local infections in vital organs. Blood poisoning, resulting from infection in the blood stream, was very common. But worst of all, and most dreaded, was hospital gangrene, an infection which literally killed the tissue around the wound and which spread rapidly through the flesh like an invading army. Amputation was the only answer, and there was no assurance that new gangrene would not start in the stump of the leg or arm. Gangrene in the upper part of the body or in vital organs was always fatal.

Epidemics of gangrene swept in waves through the best hospitals. In the worst, it was ever present.

The stench of decaying flesh filled the air. The atmosphere was almost unbearable in spite of constantly open windows.

Surgeons despaired of bettering conditions. Some said the only remedy was to tear down all the hospitals and replace them with small cottages, which would take care of no more than two patients each.

Such were the conditions of only a hundred years ago. In that day and earlier, many suffering patients chose a painful, lingering death at home rather than the horrors of the most modern hospital of their day.

All this was changed by Joseph Lister, who would have burned the surgeon's prized frock coat, even in his student days. He saw the coat as a symbol of all that was wrong in the medical customs of the times.

Joseph Lister was born in April, 1827, the son of a prosperous and wholesome Quaker family. His childhood was made pleasant by a father who gave his children loving attention while he guided their interests toward serious matters. Afternoon hikes became explorations for fossils; leisure at home be-

came times when young Joseph read Latin to his
father.

John Jackson Lister, father of Joseph, was a wine
merchant, but the microscope was his hobby, and
he became one of the developers of the present-day
compound microscope. He made his son a present
of one during Joseph's later medical-school years.
There was a deep companionship between the two
as long as John Lister lived. Even when Joseph had
become a professor of surgery his father gently rep-
rimanded him for delaying the preparation of his
lectures.

At seventeen, Joseph entered the University College of London. Almost at once he became fascinated by the immense problems of infection and inflammation. He made experiments and published a
paper reporting on studies of inflammation in the
web of a frog. While still a young student, he studied pus formation in pyemia and also an epidemic
of gangrene in the hospital wards.

After obtaining his medical degree in 1853 at the
age of twenty-six, he was persuaded to first make
a month's visit to the clinic of Professor Syme in

Edinburgh. He went, and it was a choice that changed his entire life.

In Edinburgh he found a close friend in the crusty, outspoken Syme, who was the most competent surgeon and teacher in Great Britain at the time. When the month ended, Joseph decided to stay on. Not a small part of the reason may have been Agnes Syme, the professor's young daughter. Joseph married her two and a half years later, in 1856.

As if to test Joseph, Syme gave him an inconsequential clerical job. But Joseph accepted with humility and thanks for the opportunity to observe the work of the great surgeon and study his methods. The clerical job didn't last long; Syme made him resident House Surgeon in 1854. From that post, Joseph advanced to Assistant Surgeon to the Infirmary, and lecturer in the College of Surgeons.

All his spare time was spent in studies and experiments. After their marriage, Agnes worked beside him; his extensive notes and writings are mostly in her hand.

Then, in 1860, a great opportunity came his way.

He was offered the post of Professor of Surgery at
the University of Glasgow. For the first time, he
would have full charge of a hospital ward. He was
thirty-three now, but he would have a chance at last
to see if hospital conditions could be improved!

Two nurses were talking in the corridor. "That
new Dr. Lister is going to drive us all crazy!" said
one. "These clean towels he wants in readiness all
over the place, and all this hot water! You'd think
we were running a laundry instead of a hospital."

"I know what you mean," the other replied. "He's
got so's he won't even examine two patients in a row
without washing and scrubbing his hands between
times. And he insists on putting a fresh sheet on a
bed for each new patient, even though there may be
no more than a spot or two of blood on the old
sheet."

"He'll drive us all crazy with this constant washing and changing!"

The voices of the nurses faded away down the
hall. Joseph Lister permitted himself to smile a little
as they moved away. But it was a bitter smile. Since

taking over the wards assigned to him, Joseph had set up standards of cleanliness such as had never been heard of before. His fellow surgeons laughed at his excessive washing and cleaning. The hospital managers quarreled with him because he refused to put more beds in his wards than they had been designed to hold.

All of this—and no results.

Erysipelas, pyemia, gangrene—the old hospital diseases still raged in his wards. He had been so sure that a decent amount of cleanliness would rid them of the diseases. Now his fine theory was a complete failure, and his colleagues were having a merry time at his expense. Maybe those who wanted to tear down all the hospitals in England and put up little cottages were right!

Joseph discussed the matter with anyone who would listen. "What causes these diseases?" he asked over and over again.

An older surgeon spoke kindly to him. "It's the air, especially the oxygen. It acts on the fluids in the wounds and thus generates gangrene and the other diseases. There's no prevention. You must learn to live with this condition, as we all have. You can't shut off the air!"

Another said, "It's miasms, that's all. How are you going to combat that?"

"What are miasms?" asked Joseph.

"Well—they're—" The other surgeon waved his hands helplessly. "They're just—you know—miasms. That's all you can say about them—gases in the air, if you please."

Joseph had heard the word before. He knew it was meaningless.

One afternoon in 1864 he was walking home at the end of the day with Thomas Anderson, Professor of Chemistry in Glasgow. They had been discussing the possible causes of decay in gangrenous flesh.

"I have recently read some papers by a French chemist which I think would interest you and might throw some light on your problem," said Professor Anderson. "I'll see that you get copies if you'd care to read them."

"I certainly would," said Joseph. "A French chemist, you say? What is his name?"

"Louis—Louis Pasteur. Seems to be a very brilliant fellow."

Joseph Lister had never heard of him.

He obtained copies of Louis Pasteur's papers on fermentation and spontaneous generation and read them with excitement and delight. Joseph felt a sense of deep admiration and affection for this unknown French chemist whose work was like a sudden burst of light in the vast darkness.

Miasms! Gases of the air!

Joseph knew his enemies now. Tiny living things, so small they could be borne from place to place on the dust particles of the air. Germs, Pasteur had called them. Well, germs were something a surgeon could fight!

All that was needed was a weapon.

Pasteur's methods of destroying germs included only heat, so far. Something else was needed to kill the germs in a wound. A chemical antiseptic.

About this time Joseph read in the newspapers that the nearby city of Carlisle had recently solved a problem in its sewage system. Previously, the whole city had smelled of the putrefaction of its sewage. Then, by pouring a small amount of carbolic acid into the system, all offensive odor had been destroyed.

Carbolic acid had been used before to get rid of putrefaction and decay, Joseph knew. So, if Pasteur was right, carbolic acid did its work by destroying the germs that caused decay of living matter.

It should be able to destroy them in a wound as well as in a sewer.

Eagerly, Joseph tried it on his first available case. He applied carbolic acid to a serious compound fracture—a broken bone which protruded through the flesh. This was in March, 1865. The effort was a failure. The patient died.

Joseph blamed his own mismanagement. "It's not enough to simply wash the wound with carbolic acid and kill germs that may be present at the time," he told his assistants, "just as it was not enough to provide clean dressings and bedding and instruments. What must be done is to kill the germs which are present, and keep any others from entering the wound. That is the process that will insure success!"

In August one of his assistants announced, "Dr.

Lister, a bad case of compound fracture has just come into the ward."

"All right," said Joseph quietly. "See that everything is prepared as I have instructed. This time we shall see who wins."

"I hope we are more fortunate than we were with that poor fellow last spring—"

"We shall be. We shall be."

The leg had been broken by a cart passing over it. The bone protruded through bruised and bleeding flesh. Joseph applied undiluted carbolic acid to the wound. The bone was straightened and the ends joined, ready for splints. Then gauze, dipped in carbolic acid, was laid over the wound, overlapping all around. Splints were applied, and the leg was bound up.

Four days later, Joseph opened the dressing. There was no pus formation at all.

"You see?" said Joseph to the hospital assistants. "We killed the germs in the wound with carbolic acid. Then, with the antiseptic dressing, we kept the other germs out. We will continue to keep them out until the wound is healed."

He applied another dressing prepared with diluted carbolic acid. Five days later, the deeper part of the wound was closed. Joseph used simple dressings without further antiseptic. After the bones had joined, the patient was discharged from the hospital. The whole matter of his healing had been so simple and uneventful that it was astonishing.

Joseph felt now that he knew something about combating the little killers Pasteur had discovered. But his confidence was shaken the day ten-year-old James was brought in. The boy, already a workman in a factory to help support his family, had been caught in a machine. His forearm had been torn all the way around, the muscles were slashed, and both bones broken. A splinter of bone an inch long protruded from the wound.

"The operating room is ready for amputation," said the assistants, as soon as Joseph arrived.

"Amputation? Why are you so sure we must amputate?" Joseph took off his coat and put on the clean white apron which he had introduced to the operating room to replace the old black frock coat. He washed his hands carefully in soap and water, then bathed them in carbolic acid.

"The damage can be repaired," he said confidently as he examined the unconscious boy with gentle touch. "The bones will grow together, and the muscles can be stitched in their proper places."

"But the gangrene! It will be impossible to keep the gangrene out of such a wound!"

"If we do keep it out, however, we shall know for a surety that the antiseptic system is a success, shall we not?" said Joseph.

His assistants nodded unhappily. They knew it was impossible. In such cases as this if the limb were not amputated, gangrene was almost a certainty.

The splinter of bones was cut away under anesthetic, and strips of badly torn muscle were removed. The whole wound was washed freely with undiluted carbolic acid. The bones were set, and bandages treated with carbolic acid were applied. Oiled paper was put over them to keep the antiseptic from evaporating. The wound was dressed daily with carbolic acid.

In seven weeks the miracle was complete. Young James had a whole arm again.

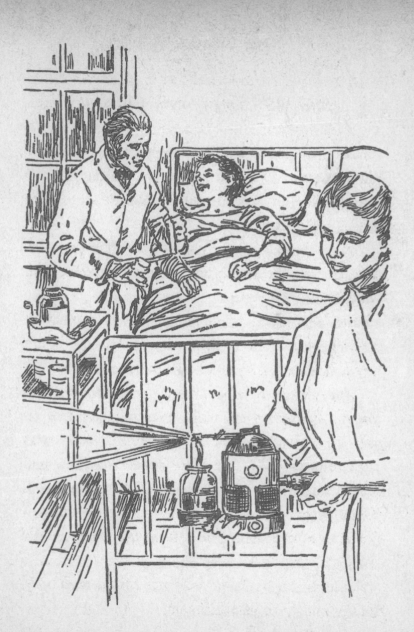

In surgery, Joseph extended the idea of carbolic acid disinfection by arranging a spray to distribute a carbolic acid mist over the wound during the entire time it was open. A small steam engine was used to pump the mist into the air. In the wards, a hand spray was pumped constantly while the dressings were being changed.

After treating eleven cases, five of which had been completely free from pus, and only one of which died, Joseph Lister wrote his results for publication and made an address to the British Medical Association.

He received the same kind of treatment other discoverers before him had been given. Most of his listeners at the medical convention laughed. Others were bored and considered him a little eccentric. "Little bugs in the air causing disease!" they scoffed. "What a fool that lunatic Frenchman has made of Joseph Lister!"

His wards at Glasgow became the talk of the medical world, however. The success of his cases could not be denied, and visitors from the continent took his ideas home and tried them. Some made halfway efforts and failed; they called Lister's system a failure. Others followed his precise directions and succeeded.

In 1869, Joseph returned to Edinburgh to take the place of his father-in-law, who had suffered a stroke. In 1876 he visited Philadelphia and was received enthusiastically by American surgeons.

By this time, most large medical centers had begun to accept and practice his methods—all except London. In 1877, he returned to the small King's College Hospital. Amid hostility from colleagues, nurses, and students alike, he began the uphill work of trying to establish his antiseptic system there.

As before, his calm, mild manner and the obvious success of his system began to win over even the strongest of his opponents. He was given the title of Baron in 1883, and was thereafter known as Lord Lister.

Joseph Lister's method was so simple and his results so amazing that it was difficult for many to understand what he had done. Antiseptics had been used before, without marked success. Why did they work for Lister?

Joseph Lister's contribution was not simply the application of antiseptics, nor cleanliness, nor any other single thing. It was a system that combined all these things and was based on Louis Pasteur's discovery of germs. Joseph saw that by killing germs that were present in a wound and keeping others from entering, the terrible hospital diseases could be prevented. His system accomplished this.

He was constantly trying to improve. He searched for better antiseptics than carbolic acid, which was harsh. By 1890 he gave up the practice of spraying the acid mist into the air of the wards and operating rooms. He had learned that the disease-bearing germs were not actually in the air so much as they were in dirt on the hands, instruments, and clothing. He practiced the sterilization of instruments and sterilized the sutures used in sewing wounds. Later, the use of rubber gloves was introduced from America. Face masks came into use to prevent the "germs" entering a wound from the breath of the surgeon and his assistants.

From Germany came the later practice of sterilizing gowns, dressings, and other articles used in the operating room. This eliminated the need for such great sterilization at the site of a wound.

These practices were all designed to reach the goal that Joseph Lister set up when he first learned of the work of Louis Pasteur: Kill the germs that are present and prevent the intrusion of others.

This is what the modern surgeon does with all his shining, sterile equipment, and his up-to-date antiseptics and antibiotics. But it was Joseph Lister who banished forever the old black frock coat and replaced it with a germ-free environment where pus and gangrene cannot thrive. He made it possible for patients to enter hospitals safely, knowing they would not be afflicted with more ills than they brought with them.

A highlight in the career of two great men of science occurred in 1892, on the seventieth birthday of Louis Pasteur. Joseph attended the great celebration. As the aged and feeble Pasteur entered the hall, Joseph Lister—only five years younger— got to his feet and rushed toward him. The two men embraced like brothers.

Later, Joseph spoke to the assembly and to

Louis Pasteur. He said, "The great honor has been accorded me of bringing you the homage of the sciences of medicine and surgery."

No two men then living had done more for the welfare of mankind than those two great scientists present on that eventful day.

In 1893, Lady Agnes Lister died of pneumonia on a vacation in Italy. Joseph lived his final years in quiet seclusion and died, laden with the honors of the world, on February 10, 1912.

11

The Path Ahead

Some of the greatest names of medical science have been mentioned in this short space, but many others could not be.

There is Morgagni in the eighteenth century, who was the first to study systematically and report on the effects of disease on the human body.

There is Robert Koch, who lived at the time of Pasteur, and who proved beyond doubt the identity of many specific organisms as the causes of disease, carrying on the work Pasteur began.

There is Sir Alexander Fleming, who gave the world penicillin and led the way to the discovery of the host of useful antibiotics known today.

There is Sigmund Freud, who opened the way to

an understanding of the workings and illnesses of the mind of man.

Scores of others remain unnamed, but the stories of those who built the foundations have been given. Yet the structure of medicine is not finished and perhaps never will be. We know a great deal about anatomy; surgical techniques are being improved daily; the conquest of disease is well along. Recent years have seen the discovery of great secrets in the chemistry of the body, and we appear to be on the threshold of understanding the intricate coding processes by which the characteristics of living things are passed from one generation to the next.

The things we don't know about ourselves and other living things, however, are staggering. We understand so little about the workings of the mind, nerves, and chemical factories of man and other creatures that at times it seems we know nothing.

In spite of how far we have come, there still remains more to be learned of the mystery of the human body than has so far been discovered in all the years since Hippocrates.

The adventure is just beginning!

Whitman
CLASSICS

Five Little Peppers Midway

Freckles

Wild Animals I Have Known

Rebecca of Sunnybrook
  Farm

Alice in Wonderland

Mrs. Wiggs of the
  Cabbage Patch

Fifty Famous Fairy Tales

Rose in Bloom

Eight Cousins

Little Women

Little Men

Five Little Peppers and
  How They Grew

Robinson Crusoe

Treasure Island

Heidi

The Call of the Wild

Tom Sawyer

Beautiful Joe

Adventures of Sherlock Holmes

Here are some of the best-loved stories of all time.
Delightful ... intriguing ... never-to-be-forgotten
tales that you will read again and again. Start
your own home library of WHITMAN CLASSICS
so that you'll always have exciting books at your
finger tips.

Whitman
REG. U.S. PAT. OFF.

Whitman ADVENTURE and MYSTERY Books

Adventure Stories for GIRLS and BOYS...

TIMBER TRAIL RIDERS
The Long Trail North
The Texas Tenderfoot
The Luck of Black Diamond

THE BOBBSEY TWINS
In the Country
Merry Days Indoors and Out
At the Seashore

DONNA PARKER
In Hollywood
At Cherrydale
Special Agent
On Her Own
A Spring to Remember
Mystery at Arawak

TROY NESBIT SERIES
The Forest Fire Mystery
The Jinx of Payrock Canyon
Sand Dune Pony

New Stories About Your Television Favorites...

Dr. Kildare
Assigned to Trouble

Janet Lennon
And the Angels
Adventure at Two Rivers
Camp Calamity

Walt Disney's Annette
The Mystery at Smugglers' Cove
The Desert Inn Mystery
Sierra Summer
The Mystery at Moonstone Bay

The Lennon Sisters
Secret of Holiday Island

Leave It to Beaver

Ripcord

The Beverly Hillbillies

Lassie
The Mystery at Blackberry Bog

Lucy
The Madcap Mystery

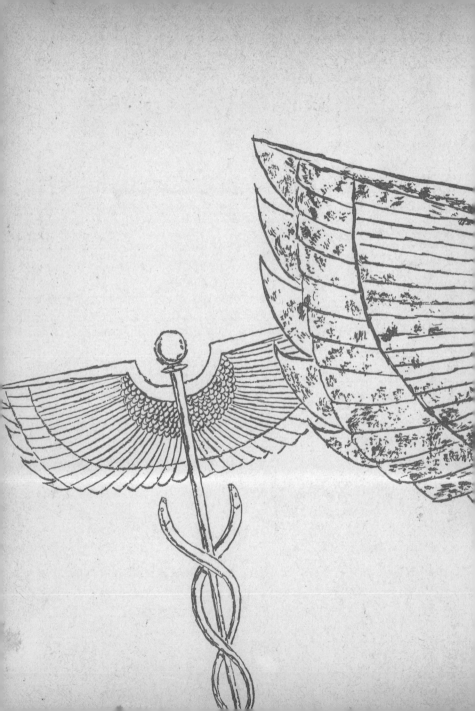